AVICENNA AND THE ARISTOTELIAN LEFT

NEW DIRECTIONS IN CRITICAL THEORY

NEW DIRECTIONS IN CRITICAL THEORY
AMY ALLEN, GENERAL EDITOR

A complete list of titles in the series begins on p. 111

AVICENNA AND THE ARISTOTELIAN LEFT

ERNST BLOCH

Translated by Loren Goldman and Peter Thompson

Columbia University Press
New York

Columbia University Press
Publishers Since 1893
New York   Chichester, West Sussex
cup.columbia.edu

Avicenna und die aristotelische Linke copyright © 1963 Suhrkamp Verlag Frankfurt am Main
All rights reserved by Suhrkamp Verlag Berlin

Copyright © 2019 Columbia University Press
All rights reserved

Library of Congress Cataloging-in-Publication Data
Names: Bloch, Ernst, 1885–1977, author.
Title: Avicenna and the Aristotelian left / Ernst Bloch ; translated by Loren Goldman and Peter Thompson.
Other titles: Avicenna und die aristotelische Linke. English
Description: New York : Columbia University Press, 2018. | Includes bibliographical references and index.
Identifiers: LCCN 2018010142 | ISBN 9780231175340 (cloth) | ISBN 9780231175357 (pbk.) | ISBN 9780231548144 (ebook) Subjects: LCSH: Avicenna, 980–1037. | Aristotle. | Materialism. Classification: LCC B751.Z7 B5613 2018 | DDC 181/.5—dc23
LC record available at https://lccn.loc.gov/2018010142

Cover design: Milenda Nan Ok Lee

Cover art: copyright © Shutterstock

CONTENTS

A Note on the Text and Translation   vii
Acknowledgments   ix
Introduction   xi
    LOREN GOLDMAN

Avicenna and the Aristotelian Left   1

Notes   69
Bibliography   95
Index   105

A NOTE ON THE TEXT AND TRANSLATION

Originally composed for the journal *Sinn und Form*,[1] *Avicenna and the Aristotelian Left* was expanded for publication as a monograph by Rütten & Loening publishers (1952) and slightly revised as an appendix to *Das Materialismusproblem: seine Geschichte und Substanz* (1972).[2] This translation follows the latter edition's text as published in volume 7 of Bloch's *Gesamtausgabe* (1977).[3] Page numbers to the *Gesamtausgabe* version are noted in square brackets.

Avicenna and the Aristotelian Left comprises a historical monograph on Avicenna's legacy and a long appendix entitled "Textual Passages and Annotations." The latter, a collection of primary sources along with Bloch's commentaries, is integral to the whole. When the book was published, many of these texts were difficult to find, and several remain so: a passage from Bruno's "The Awakener,"[4] for example, appears here for the first time in English. We have reproduced standard English translations where available, noting when they diverge from Bloch's sources. An idiosyncratic difficulty that we faced is that Bloch's German translation of Avicenna's *Metaphysics*, by Max Horten (1907), follows a different source manuscript than the

English translation by Michael Marmura (2005); in the interest of full disclosure, variant readings are given in the notes.[5]

We have aimed for a balance between clarity, readability, and accuracy in capturing Bloch's unique voice. Bloch was a notoriously obscure author, whose writing can be fiendishly tricky even for native German speakers as his style combines dialectical logic and poetic expression with a surprising informality. The reader should keep in mind that he does not sound "normal" to German ears. Given the subject matter, the era, and the subject position of its author, it is no surprise that Bloch occasionally employs Orientalist language that is no longer accepted in academic writing. While nothing here is patently offensive, we have left the text unsanitized; Bloch's deep appreciation for the philosophical contributions of Avicenna and his intellectual descendants should be clear. We follow Bloch's language throughout, for example, mirroring his use of the names "Avicenna" and "Ibn Sina" and preserving his choices of "Oriental" and "Eastern" (which he uses neutrally and interchangeably). Central concepts and thorny phrases are given in the notes in the original German. Finally, instead of footnotes, the German text has parenthetical comments, many of which we moved to the notes. To differentiate these from our annotations, Bloch's notes are marked in **bold**.

ACKNOWLEDGMENTS

This edition of *Avicenna and the Aristotelian Left* would not have been possible without the generosity and expertise of many colleagues. We thank Amy Allen, Osman Balkan, Neil Bernstein, Stephen Bronner, Christopher Buck, Scott Carson, Julie Cooper, Rita Copeland, Mihaela Czobor-Lupp, Eva Del Soldato, Marsha Dutton, Jamal Elias, Ottmar Ette, Matthew Evangelista, Kyle Jones, Ken Garden, Jake Greear, Dimitri Gutas, Andree Hahmann, Gunnar Hindrichs, Martin Jay, Nicole Kaufman, Joseph Lowry, Loren Lybarger, Jon McGinnis, Susan Sauvé Meyer, Anne Norton, Johan Siebers, Troels Skadhauge, Steven Tester, Kirk Wetters, Lawrence Wittner, and Slavoj Žižek. At Columbia University Press, we thank Wendy Lochner, Christine Dunbar, and Lowell Frye. Special thanks, finally, to Frank Degler, Roland Koch, and Klaus Kuhfeld of the Ernst Bloch Center and Archive in Ludwigshafen, Germany, who were wonderfully welcoming during a research visit and gave sage advice at several crucial moments in the translating process. Needless to say, any errors in the text are ours alone.

INTRODUCTION

Loren Goldman

Avicenna and the Aristotelian Left, Ernst Bloch's study of the thinker he affectionately called "my friend Ibn Sina,"[1] does many things. Most evidently, it traces a concept of vital materialism from Aristotle to Karl Marx—one developed by medieval Islamic philosophers Avicenna (980–1037) and Averroës (1126–1198), Jewish Andalusian poet-philosopher Avicebron (c. 1021–1070), and Renaissance pantheist Giordano Bruno (1548–1600) along with other major and minor figures—that ultimately informs Bloch's strikingly unorthodox materialist worldview. In addition to offering an unsurpassed précis of Bloch's own speculative materialism, it also presents itself as a testament to Bloch's extraordinary learning and imaginative genius; as early as 1952, he was insisting on the intertwined nature of Arabic and Western thought in the medieval period and beyond, a perspective that has only become common among specialists in the field in recent years.[2] Moreover, by situating the world's emancipatory possibilities in the Islamic interpretation of Aristotle, this small book provides a provocative reconstruction of the sources of modern philosophy that both confounds standard binaries of East/West and Premodernity/Modernity and makes a strong case for the ongoing relevance of metaphysics for contemporary critical theory. For Bloch, the issues raised in this volume resonate far beyond the bounds of scholarship as Avicenna's legacy lights a path for inquiry about the very compatibility of utopia and reality. In the works of Avicenna and Averroës, thinkers living nearly a millennium before him, Bloch detects the seeds of a lively view of matter that permits and even invites utopian aspiration.

Despite being one of the most consequential German philosophers of the twentieth century,[3] Bloch (1885–1977) remains in the shadows of better-known contemporaries such as Georg Lukács, Theodor Adorno, Max Horkheimer, and Walter Benjamin, all of whom were his friends. Reasons for this neglect involve both his substance and his style. Bloch's unapologetic embrace of utopianism and his willingness to seriously engage religion often led to the assumption that his work suffers from mystification, that it is fixated on epiphenomenal appearances instead of essential reality. Thus, Max Scheler wrote that Bloch seemed to be "running amok to God"; Siegfried Kracauer complained that he was "fornicating with God"; and Max Weber reportedly described his relationship to Bloch tartly: "He is possessed by his God, and I am a scientist."[4] Moreover, for the work of an avowed Marxist, not to mention one of the few notable postwar German intellectuals who chose to live in East Germany,[5] Bloch's writings can seem detached from the materialism that is so central to that tradition. His effusive commentaries on Western opera, Chinese fairy tales, and the ancient Egyptian pantheon can overwhelm his dutiful references to economic structures and modes of production. The fact that most of Bloch's work available in English translation concerns aesthetics, culture, and the utopian content of religion can leave his non-German readers with the mistaken impression that he is uninterested in deeper ontological questions.[6] *Avicenna and the Aristotelian Left* puts paid to this misapprehension, showing Bloch's investment in an account of a material reality in which the possibility of radical social transformation grows in the latent tendencies of matter itself.

Bloch's utopianism and his interest in aesthetic and religious forms of expression partly explain the relative neglect of his work, but his style admittedly serves as another barrier, for his impressive scope is matched only by the difficulty of his writing. The famously abstruse Adorno wrote an essay entitled "*Grosse Blochmusik*" (great Bloch music), a pun on *Blechmusik* (brass-band music, a title composed with a wink, as *Blech* can also mean "nonsense"), and said that *The Spirit of Utopia* seemed to have been written "by Nostradamus himself."[7] Similarly, Jürgen Habermas described Bloch as giving philosophical representation to late expressionism, with its "exploded fragments of a hyphenated terminology, the welling exuberance of a pleonastic phraseology, the strong-chested breathing of dithyrambic plangency."[8] Bloch indeed demands an active reader, perhaps because his writing unfolds according to his notion of the basic human condition: the essential darkness of our lived present is illuminated in flashes by the *not yet* of utopian consciousness. In any event, Adorno, Habermas, and countless others have found the effort of reading Bloch worthwhile.

BLOCH'S PHILOSOPHY OF HOPE

Because Bloch's general philosophical concerns are hope and utopia, understanding his intellectual project is helpful background for *Avicenna and the Aristotelian Left*. Scheler's and Kracauer's quips reflect the perennial suspicion of unreality that confronts utopian thinking. This challenge is, of course, reflected in the word "utopia," coined by Thomas More by joining the Greek οὐ (*ou*: no, not) with τόπος (*topos*: place), yielding "no-place," a convenient homonym of εὐ-τόπος (*eu-topos*), "good-place"; More's narrator, not coincidentally, is named Hytholyday, "nonsense-peddler."[9] Hope poses a similar problem, for it orients us toward an uncertain future and toward imaginary constructs that may threaten to distract from the exigencies of the present. And although hope now has a generally positive valence,[10] the ancient Greeks viewed it with ambivalence: in myth, Pandora kept hope from escaping its home in her jar of *evils*,[11] and the epithet most commonly associated with it was "blind."

Bloch does consider hope to be a basic principle of human experience, but he does not suggest its blind embrace or that we hope willy-nilly *for anything*. Rather than being entranced by reality's mystical shell, Bloch focuses his attention on aesthetics and religion in order to reveal what he believes to be their secular and human inner utopian core, the germ of real longing for what he called "the fulfilled moment" of genuine emancipation.[12] The beatific state spells a qualitative transfiguration in human relations, and Bloch calls it the *Novum*, or the genuinely novel, to distinguish it from the *Neue*, or the new that we have come to expect, a new that is merely a repetition of the old—a "new and improved" blender, for instance.[13] The cultural products of human expression are not (merely) epiphenomenal echoes of material dynamics but rather provide "anticipations" (*Vorscheine*: "pre-appearances") of utopian possibilities. While it is true in one sense to say that utopia does not exist, Bloch insists on a further qualification: utopia does *not yet* exist. In another sense, then, utopia is real, albeit latent and in process. As Bloch explains, "So far does utopia extend, so vigorously does this raw material spread to all human activities, so essentially must every anthropology and science of the world contain it. *There is no realism worthy of the name if it abstracts from this strongest element in reality, as an unfinished reality*."[14] Because reality is always in the process of becoming, utopian aspiration may have traction and may even aid in the utopia's realization. Ultimately, and notably in the closing chapters of *The Spirit of Utopia* and *The Principle of Hope*, Bloch attributes reality's processual nature to Marx's basic insight that human labor produces and reproduces the world, thereby (in Bloch's reading) identifying free, creative agency as the motor of historical development.

Many futures lie dormant in the present, however, and not just any of them can, should, or will come to fruition. How to distinguish between effective utopias and pipe dreams becomes a crucial part of Bloch's project, and he divides utopia and hope alike into "abstract" and "concrete" species. Simply put, an abstract utopia is unrealizable while a concrete utopia is realizable. Unlike an abstract utopia, a concrete utopia is predicated on an understanding of reality's underlying tendencies—a technical term in Bloch, meaning "the energy of matter in action."[15] This distinction is central, for Bloch viewed himself as a partisan of a concrete utopia and inveighed against an abstract utopia as passionately as his own critics attacked him. When Bloch explains that he wants his readers to "learn to hope,"[16] he means both that they must grasp their utopian aspirations as essential to their selves *and* that they must come to discern and embrace concrete utopia.

Bloch's understanding that concrete utopia reflects active tendencies in the world is further illuminated by his description of the various "layers" of possibility, particularly his distinction between what he calls "the fact-based object-suited possible" and "the objectively-real possible" or "real possibility."[17] The first relates to what is considered possible *given the present worldly state of affairs*; the second relates to what is possible *given the latent tendencies of the world and the fact of ongoing human agency*. From the first perspective, motorized travel was impossible in ancient Babylonia and medieval Strasbourg alike, as both the technology and the know-how to create it were lacking. From the second perspective, however, motorized travel was always possible, but the tools to bring it to fruition had not yet been harnessed. The first type of possibility, in other words, reflects the current state of knowledge about the world; the second type, by contrast, reflects the fact that new facets of the world regularly come into being. Bloch holds, finally, that modern science trucks solely with the first type of possibility, in which the present constellation of facts is accepted as immutable. To this, he contrasts a "Real possibility" that takes stock of the forces operating in the process of becoming, chief among which is human freedom in fashioning self and world. As Bloch put it, reality consists of "the events produced by working people together with the abundant interweaving process-connections between past, present, and future."[18] Thus, utopian thought presupposes a world capable of being radically different from its current state. Bloch accordingly saw the need for an account of the latent potential of the world that allows us to envision the growth of genuinely new social forms out of our material existence without the aid of the supernatural. The explanation and possibility of concrete hope lead Bloch to the philosophy of nature in general and to the concept of matter in particular.[19]

UTOPIA AND DIALECTICAL MATTER

The Avicennan narrative notwithstanding, Bloch's reflections on the philosophy of nature grew more immediately out of the *Materialismusstreit*, a debate in nineteenth-century German letters about whether matter was inert or self-generating, a controversy that revived the determinism/freedom and theism/pantheism controversies of the eighteenth century in the language of then-contemporary science.[20] Friedrich Engels's and Vladimir Lenin's respective interventions, *Anti-Dühring* and *Dialectics of Nature* on the one hand and *Materialism and Empirio-Criticism* on the other,[21] indicate the interest this question held for followers of Marx, whose first thesis on Feuerbach calls for a materialism that recognizes reality not merely as an object of contemplation but as "sensuous human activity, practice."[22] The early Marx also served as an inspiration for Bloch, who sought to make sense of Marx's description of a society free from alienation as "the essential unity of man and nature, ... the genuine resurrection of nature, the accomplished naturalism of man and the accomplished humanism of nature."[23] This glimpse of utopia suggests a world in which human activity is, as Bloch later described it, "co-productive" with nature.[24] Such a state of affairs would signal the end of humanity's exploitative relationship to nature—a relationship Bloch associated with capitalism—and mark the beginning of a collaborative one that would entail (again following early Marx) the end of the alienation of humanity from nature and, by extension, of humanity from itself.[25] Such an emancipated world would, indeed, be genuinely unprecedented—*Novum*, not merely *Neue*—and so Bloch argues that we need an account of matter that permits truly novel possibilities.

Bloch rejects what he considers to be the "narrow, ossified" view of matter in modern science,[26] writing, "Mechanical materialism can have no utopia. Everything is present in it, mechanically present."[27] In failing to acknowledge reality as unfinished, the mechanistic view threatens utopia altogether. If matter is fixed, change becomes unthinkable, and hope pointless—put in Bloch's terms, mechanistic matter makes utopia "abstract." Bloch thus worries that "confronted with the future-state which stands like an agreed consequence in the so-called iron logic of history, the subject can just as easily lay his hands in his lap as he once folded them when confronted with God's will."[28] Instead, we need to think of the world as becoming, for only when possibilities remain latent is it possible to imagine the realization of a "concrete" utopia. A world of becoming requires a dynamic conception of matter, however, which allows "new shoots and new spaces for development" against the completed world of inert matter.[29] To invoke Bloch's aforementioned layers of possibility, mechanism reflects "the fact-based object-suited possible," while dialectical matter alone is able to convey the Real possibility of a concrete utopia in process.

Bloch calls his conception of matter "neo-Aristotelian," and Aristotle's discussion in the *Metaphysics* provides the four key terms for Bloch's own analysis: matter, form, potentiality and actuality.[30] For Aristotle, all subjects are compounds of matter and form, the former providing the material (say, wood), and the latter providing the essential substance (say, chairness or bedness);[31] Aristotle privileges form because it lends the thing its essence—a bed is a bed whether made out of wood or metal. There is a closely linked distinction in Aristotle between potentiality (δύναμις, *dynamis*) and actuality (ενέργεια, *energeia*, or ἐντελέχεια, *entelechia*).[32] Matter exists in a state of potentiality—it has the capacity to become many things—which attains actuality when combined with form.[33] The precise relationship between matter, form, potentiality, and actuality has been a source of debate among Aristotle scholars from his earliest commentators in the ancient world to philosophers of the present day.

Bloch's interpretation mobilizes the ambiguity of matter's potentiality against the primacy of form that Aristotle implies. Bloch finds in Aristotle's *dynamis* both structured and unstructured types of potentiality, which are differentiated by their capacity to receive form. The first, structured type of potentiality, *kata to dynaton*, Bloch renders as *Nach-Möglichkeit-Sein*; the second, unstructured type, *dynamei-on*, Bloch renders as *In-Möglichkeit-Sein*. Literally translated, these terms become "Being-According-to-Possibility" and "Being-in-Possibility," a distinction as confusing in English as it is in German. Peter Thompson and I have opted instead for "what-is-considered-possible" and "what-may-become-possible." The latter phrases more clearly convey Bloch's meaning, which can be gleaned by reference, again, to the layers of possibility. What-is-considered-possible, the kata to dynaton, denotes that which is possible given what we know now while what-may-become-possible, the dynamei-on, is that which may become possible whether or not it accords with currently accepted notions of possibility. For Bloch, this fecund material basis of form approximates the real objectivity whereby reality is inscribed in the process of becoming. To put this explanation in more concrete terms, in the ancient world, a world without slavery would have been considered impossible by most, for the institution and the assumption of natural inferiority that underlay it were widespread. To argue for its end would have seemed foolishly utopian, for, in a refrain one still hears constantly, that was just the way things were. And yet the abolition of slavery was possible (had there been the will to abolish it) and remains so today; it is not a natural fact that humans *must* be enslaved to other humans even if it is an undeniable and morally abhorrent reality that human beings have been so enslaved since time immemorial. To look to what-may-become-possible rather than just what-is-considered-possible is to appreciate the possible that transcends the bounds of accepted possibility, the possibility that there are possibilities we have not yet actualized; this is why Bloch prefers the more "open" possibility of the Aristotelian dynamei-on.

This openness is crucial for Bloch's concept of matter and for his thought as a whole—he regularly called his philosophical project an "open system."[34] It is reflected, furthermore, not only in his preferred understanding of potentiality in the dynamei-on but also in his preferred understanding of actuality, the *energia* or *entelechy*. In Aristotle, entelechy is the principle that propels something's development from potential to actuality. This is almost always toward a determinate end, leading to the formal development of matter into particularly predisposed shapes, an entelechy whose telos is defined and whose realization will spell the actualization of said telos in the world. Bloch, however, draws on a different type of entelechy that Aristotle mentions—"open," "incomplete," or "unfinished entelechy"—and occasionally uses this phrase to define his notion of matter.[35] For Aristotle, unfinished entelechy describes progress in motion: the entelechy of a train approaching Philadelphia, for example. Bloch interprets unfinished entelechy as being related not only to motion but also to ends themselves, for—in his view, at least—matter itself is in the process of development. What develops it, moreover, is human agency, itself rooted in openness by dint of the human capacity for freedom.

It may be helpful, finally, to add one last distinction. Bloch sees Marxism as a story of the fruitful interaction of a scientific, analytical impulse and a visionary, utopian impulse. These "cold" and "warm" streams of Marxism represent complementary needs: the former combats Jacobinism and extravangantism while the latter combats "the danger of economism and of goal-forgetting opportunism."[36] As Bloch sees it, his doctrine of coldness relates to what-is-considered-possible, operating with a conventional understanding of possibility. His doctrine of warmth, by contrast, is "solely related to that positive what-may-become-possible, not subject to any disenchantment, which embraces the growing realization and the realizing element, primarily in the human sphere."[37] "Dialectical matter" is what Bloch's ontology ultimately seeks to illuminate, a negotiation between the poles of coldness and warmth, between the kata to dynaton and the dynamei-on, between the categories of what-is-considered-possible and what-may-become-possible, as it is realized in concert with human action.

AVICENNA AND THE ARISTOTELIAN LEFT

Avicenna and the Aristotelian Left is Bloch's first published work dedicated to materialism. Although it appeared in 1952, its origins date back decades earlier: in 1936 Bloch sent Horkheimer a letter enthusiastically describing a notebook he had compiled of passages from energetic materialists, including Averroës, Avicebron, and Giordano Bruno, which he hoped to publish with an introduction.[38] Both the compilation and the manuscript for *Avicenna* are now lost, but the present work presumably has its roots in that early project; this origin would also explain the book's unusual structure, a twenty-one-thousand-word essay followed by an extensively annotated collection of primary sources that is nearly half that length. *Avicenna and the Aristotelian Left* provides a summary of Bloch's metaphysics, but as its title suggests, his main goal in the work is to identify and revive the materialism he finds in a particular interpretation of Aristotle derived from medieval Islamic philosophy in contrast to what he perceives to be the dominant idealism of the West deriving from the Aristotelianism of Christian Scholastics such as Albertus Magnus and Thomas Aquinas.

The general contours of the story can be put succinctly. As Bloch understands the tradition, the dominant interpretation of the form-matter relationship characterizes form as the essential element that is impressed upon matter, thereby relegating nature to a passive and subordinate element in the world. For Bloch, this interpretation bespeaks a fixed world in which ideas are sovereign at the expense of concrete reality, labor is institutionally denigrated, and clerical authority is made absolute. Bloch calls this strand of thought "right-wing" Aristotelianism. Against this interpretation, Bloch sees a "left-wing" version of Aristotle that gives matter its due, supposing it to be not passive but an active collaborator without which form has no traction. He traces this tradition of Aristotle interpretation through Islamic philosophy, and he sees its seeds being laid by Avicenna before it comes to maturity in Averroës and reaches its apotheosis in Renaissance pantheism.

In "Aristotle-Avicenna and the Essences of this World," the book's central conceptual section, Bloch specifies the three main tendencies characterizing the Avicennan-Aristotelian Left. Avicenna's first major innovation was in arguing that because the body does not outlive death, the soul cannot be seen as sentient. As Bloch sees things, this philosophical step removed the "metaphysical whip" of the notion of hell in both Christianity and Islam, thereby undercutting clerical authorities' greatest weapon for keeping the masses subordinate: fear of eternal punishment. The second tendency concerns Averroës's teachings on the unity of human intellect. As Bloch reads them, Avicenna and Averroës both refuse to restrict reason to a cognitive elite, situating its capacity instead in all human beings as possible participants in active intellect. This move, too, democratizes access to truth, contrasting it against an Aristotelian Right that claimed privileged epistemological insight. The third and final tendency takes up the bulk of Bloch's reflections: the reshaping of the relationship between form and matter. Aristotle, Bloch explains, had written of a prime matter out of which anything could be formed, which contains only "passive" potentiality and hence exists incompletely. Everything that exists is a combination of this matter and form, however; as such, it has something collaborative about it. Aquinas and the Aristotelian Right emphasized the externality of form to matter, thereby making the active component in the combination something that is brought to or impressed upon matter from the outside, in this case by God and, by extension, absolute clerical-cum-political authority. By contrast, Bloch reads Avicenna and the Aristotelian Left as espying active or effective form *within* matter. The Aristotelian Left allowed that matter might be predisposed in certain ways, which Bloch interprets as opening up the space of allowing the world upon which we have imposed a particular way to be different than it actually appears. The political importance of this transformation of Aristotle maps onto the distinction between Bloch's layers of possibility: *perhaps* the world is not fixed according to the categories that God or some supernatural being has imposed upon it (as the Right Aristotelians claim), and instead human agency can educe different ways of being out of them (as the Left Aristotelians claim). The world may be pregnant with new forms that we have not yet discerned and developed.

The concluding section of the work makes a sharp turn toward poiesis, hinting at the reason aesthetics took up so much of Bloch's intellectual energies: art enables us to glimpse the "excerpt shapes" of our potential futures. This final section's expressive original title, "*Kunst, die Stoff-Form entbindend*," is difficult to render in English. *Entbinden* means both "to unbind" and "to birth," and hence, art is portrayed as something that can deliver form from matter's womb; one could as easily write that Bloch intends art to birth, or emancipate, matter *and* form. At first glance, this is identical to a solution often found in the writings of contemporaries like Theodor Adorno and Herbert Marcuse, both of whom saw art as a potential site for resisting the hyperrationalization of instrumental reason under capitalism.[39] Bloch differs from his aesthetically minded Frankfurt contemporaries insofar as he allows art a positive function in realizing the future. In practice, both Adorno's elite aesthetics of emancipation and Marcuse's "Great Refusal" are difficult to distinguish from quietist resignation in which resistance is manifested by a rejection of the contemporary world. By allowing art to trace the utopian future within matter, Bloch, by contrast, encourages his readers to grasp its latent possibilities. For this reason, art offers a model of the future not merely as a dream image but, as he writes in *The Principle of Hope*, a "pre-appearance, circulating in turbulent existence itself, of what is real."[40]

Bloch acknowledges that *Avicenna and the Aristotelian Left* is not meant to be a definitive study of Avicenna, and specialist readers of topics he discusses will undoubtedly find fault with certain aspects of his presentation.[41] For this reason, it is all the more important to remember that Bloch does not aim to give a scrupulous scholarly treatment; rather, he *means* to offer a tendentious interpretation. The work is (benignly?) tendentious in the normal sense of reflecting its author's particular ethical and political commitments, and Bloch's idiosyncratic perspectives on utopia and Marxism indisputably color all his writing. Yet *Avicenna and the Aristotelian Left* is also tendentious in a more literal and less pejorative sense: it illuminates *tendencies* in bygone thought that can only be properly grasped from a later temporal perspective. Bloch's investigation of Avicenna and others as progenitors of self-germinating matter thereby enacts what it claims to discover in those thinkers; it draws out the latent tendencies of Avicenna and his intellectual descendants for present emancipatory needs. Put otherwise, Bloch's treatment of the conceptual matter of Avicenna mirrors the Avicennans' treatment of physical matter in Aristotle, invigorating it with possibilities that its original author may have overlooked.

Attentive readers will notice that Bloch's exposition reflects this attempt to reveal the tendencies that are at play within the natural and social world and that rarely creep into consciousness. For one, the work's curious structure mirrors the texts he tackles, with a substantive primary monographical discussion followed by a compendium of annotated passages from relevant authors. In what may be a nod to his notion of the noncontemporaneity of the contemporaneous,[42] Bloch revives the medieval practice of gloss traditions that assemble and comment on writings of accepted past authorities.[43] Bloch's language in *Avicenna and the Aristotelian Left* also embeds the social world within matter. In the big picture, this is mundanely evident in the text's Marxist insistence on the rootedness of ideas in concrete material foundations: Arabic philosophy comes into being, on Bloch's reading, thanks to the vivacity of commerce; Stoicism's approach to universal reason "reflected the melting pot of the Roman Empire";[44] and orthodoxy gains the upper hand as the latter's commercial fortunes decline. More granularly, Bloch's language paints a world teeming with fecundity and dynamism, one which is often difficult to translate into English: not only does art "birth" what inheres, but remembering Avicenna is "due" (as in pregnancy), the manufacturing sector of the medieval Islamic lands was "blossoming," cloister schools "spawned" universities, Eastern reason "aborted" the letter of the text, tendencies "showed themselves" without any assistance from without, a feudal-clerical damper "laid itself atop" a vibrant materialism, the form-matter relationship itself "ripened," and things do not "begin" but are rather "put in motion." In short, the world of *Avicenna and the Aristotelian Left* is literally animated.

Its stylistic virtues aside, the substance of *Avicenna and the Aristotelian Left* is insightful and provocative. Already noted is the fact that long before the recent recovery of Islamic and Jewish thought from the shadows of Christian Scholasticism, Bloch wrote a brief for understanding the latter as deeply marked by the former. Bloch's naturalistic turn also foreshadowed the even more recent reinvigoration of matter as a conceptual concern for political philosophy and the philosophy of science. To speak of matter as a "womb of nature" will be suggestive to those taken with Gilles Deleuze's rhizomatic worlds and Hannah Arendt's conception of freedom as natality, and Bloch's insistence on reality in the process of becoming intersects with the emergent approaches to matter found in the work of William Connolly, Jane Bennett, and other contemporary vital materialists just as it intersects in significant ways with theorists of object-oriented ontology like Graham Harman and Timothy Morton and with assemblage theorists like Bruno Latour and Manuel Delanda.[45] Furthermore, Bloch's identification of an Aristotelian Left has much in common with the "aleatory materialism" of another iconoclastic Marxist philosopher, Louis Althusser, whose late writings sketch a "materialism of the encounter" that he similarly locates in an "underground current" of thought leading up to Marxism.[46] In philosophy of science, finally, something akin to Bloch's neo-Aristotelian conception of matter also has its adherents. Nobel Prize–winning physicist Ilya Prigogine and philosopher

Isabelle Stengers have written that it has become evident to modern scientists that "the natural contains essential elements of randomness and irreversibility. This leads to a new view of matter in which matter is no longer the passive substance described in the mechanistic world view but is associated with spontaneous activity." This transformation in thinking about matter allows us, they continue in the vein of Bloch (albeit without mentioning him), to "really speak about a new dialogue of man with nature."[47]

Critical questions abound, of course, although it is beyond the remit of an introduction to address them in detail. One issue involves who (or what) exactly might be the agent of the eduction of form out of matter. Alfred Schmidt's trenchant criticism of Bloch came along this line; he saw Bloch as foolishly introducing a nonhuman natural subject into his vision of a world that is pregnant with possibilities, and this invention of a *natura naturans*, he claims, far from being the contribution to dialectical materialism that Bloch thought it was, "leads directly away from it" insofar as it reduces the human transformation of nature to a subordination to the latter.[48] This worry leads to another concern, namely that if matter *does* possess latent tendencies, how exactly does one discern them or—assuming that there are multiple possibilities in the dynamei-on—distinguish between them? To put this point another way using Bloch's categories, how does one distinguish the "not yet" from the "not" and the "never"? Art might very well describe, sketch, or enable us to espy a bright alternative future, but it can also just as easily bring us to entertain fantasies whose pursuit might lead to oppression. Without dismissing this important concern as unfounded, Bloch might respond that it ultimately misses the significance of his call to rethink the matter of our facts. The point is to prepare the world and *us* for the possibility of something new, to keep the possibility of a better world *alive*. To accept only the kata to dynaton is to resign ourselves to the prospect that the world's potential is exhausted and that things will remain as they are. Bloch's emphasis on the inexhaustible, if improbable, creativity of the category of dynamei-on directs our vision to the fact that the world *does* change: the Roman

Empire fell, polio was (largely) conquered, and the category of morally equal "human" has (conceptually) expanded beyond white, male, Christian property owners. The bounds of the possible have transformed and will continue to transform, and human agency has, in fact, drawn these new possibilities out of the potential that is latent in the world.

In a 1972 letter to Bloch, economist Adolph Lowe asked in regard to a neo-Aristotelian matter, a revolutionary matter, "Who is now really the completer [*Vollzieher*] of this process, after the proletarian has become a false myth? What has become of the basic dynamics of the historical process, since recent technology has led in all areas to a pseudoempire of freedom on this side of the revolution—put another way: what is revolution today?" In response to this all-important question, Bloch demurs, saying that the two will discuss it in person, and yet he remarks (also with a wink), "I believe in surprises."[49] Even if a neo-Aristotelian conception of matter cannot ultimately answer all our queries, and even if it raises new ones in the process, it may nonetheless permit us, too, to believe in surprises.

AVICENNA AND THE ARISTOTELIAN LEFT

[479] Development is eductio formarum ex materia.
AVICENNA—AVERROËS

NEVER THE SAME

Every great idea may already have been thought seven times. But when it is thought again, in other times and places, it is never the same. Not only those who think great things but also the thought itself has meanwhile changed. The great idea has to prove itself again both in its own right and as something new. This was especially the case for the great Oriental thinkers. They simultaneously rescued and transformed the Greek light.

A POINT OF NOTE AND CONTEMPLATION

One of the earliest and greatest of these thinkers was Ibn Sina, latinized as Avicenna.[1] Born in 980 in Afshana, near Bukhara,[2] he was an ethnic Tajik. Abu Ali al-Hussein ibn Abdallah ibn Sina came from a wealthy household. His early adolescence was a healthy one, and his parents provided him with a meticulous education that corresponded to his specific talents, which emerged just at the right time to enable him to follow a clearly defined path. Well instructed in arithmetic, geometry, logic, and astronomy, he then studied philosophy and medicine,[3] and at the age of eighteen, he was able to simultaneously pursue political activities and medical science. He later became vizier to the prince of Hamadan (the ancient Ecbatana),[4] entered service with the prince of Esfahan, and after the former conquered the latter, returned to Hamadan. Beginning with fortuitously healing Nuh ibn-Mansur, the emir of Bukhara, he acquired early medical fame and with it great wealth.[5] His enemies, of which Ibn Sina [480] had many in clerical circles from the start, report that he was also keen on an excess of love and wine, which, if true, only reinforces his image as a man of strong constitution. His true excess, however, is that of his extensive writings, ninety-nine volumes of which he left to posterity.[6] Equally at home in the medical arts and philosophy, he wrote the famous *Canon of Medicine*, which served for many centuries in the East and the West alike as the standard work of medical practice.[7] His main philosophical work carries the noteworthy title *Kitab al-Shifa*, or *Book of Healing*, in which the healing of the body is linked to the power of the mind. The *Book of Healing* is an encyclopedia that deals in eighteen books with four main branches of knowledge: logic, physics, mathematics, and metaphysics. Latin versions (already in partial translations from the eleventh and twelfth centuries) are available to us: *Compendium de Anima*, *De Almahad*, *Aphorismi de Anima*, *Tractatus de Definitionibus et Quaesitis*, and *De Divisionibus Scientiarum* as well as the tracts grouped as *Metaphysika*. Lost to us now, and only known indirectly though the writings of later philosophers, is perhaps his most unorthodox work, the *Philosophia Orientalis*. Equally unorthodox (because of its language, it was known to only a small number of people) is an earlier two-volume encyclopedia, written in Tajik, known as the *Danish-Nameh* (book of knowledge), which was published in 1937–38 in Tehran.[8] Avicenna died in Esfahan in 1037 and was buried in Hamadan, where his grave can still be seen today. In 1952, answering the call of the Iranian Peace Committee,[9] Hamadan held a commemoration of the great philosopher—who belongs to the broad and progressive culture of the Near East, with its Iranian-Arabic brilliance. This thousand-year anniversary does not, indeed, accord with the European calendar but with the Islamic lunar one. And it is long overdue that European chronology more accurately acknowledge its debt to Oriental Scholasticism. For it is—in great contrast to much Western thought—one of the sources [481] of our Enlightenment and, above all, as we shall see, of a most singular materialist vitality, developed out of Aristotle in a non-Christian manner. There is a line that leads from Aristotle, not to Thomas Aquinas and to the spirit of the beyond, but to Giordano Bruno and the *blossoming* nature of universal matter. And it is Avicenna who, along with Averroës, is one of the first and most important points of note in this tradition. The purpose of the commemoration this year is to remember precisely this point.[10] And it is to be hoped that it will not simply pass into history like so many others. On the contrary, this remembrance is fitting and necessary: a long-forgotten but freshly renewed view of matter is up for debate.[11] This view reveals itself to be neither as flat as that of the mechanists nor as misplaced as that desired by those fixated on the beyond.[12] No, Avicenna handed it on to us, laden with energy.

MERCHANT CITIES AND HELLENISTIC FOUNDATIONS

Ibn Sina was a doctor, not a monk. He was as little a monk as the other significant Islamic thinkers who lived in the world and thought scientifically. Yes, the whole of Islamic society, despite its feudal forms and its spiritual wars, was organized according to a different principle than that of medieval Europe. It was, in its own way, a type of early bourgeois society with a clan structure, yet one in which mercantile capital dominated and determined social life. Mecca, the birthplace of Islam, was an ancient great emporium, one of the entrepots for trade between Arabia, Persia, India, and the Mediterranean lands. Already, long before Muhammad, only a small fraction of Arabs lived in nomadic desert tribes. There had long been Bedouin groups with agriculture, and the caravans connected the markets; Muhammad himself married into one of the most powerful of the merchant families. In Roman times, the marketplace of Mecca had been preceded by the Arab-populated trading centers of Petra and Bosra.[13] And a few years after Muhammad's death, Caliph

Umar founded the harbor at Basra, bringing shipping in the whole of the Persian Gulf under Arab influence.[14] One can thus say *cum grano salis* [482] that the Arab world had its Venices and Milans five hundred years before Europe.[15] At the same time that those parts of Europe that had been under Roman rule returned to agriculture, mercantile capital—the oldest and freest form of capital—prevailed in the Orient. In less than one hundred years after the Hijra,[16] it had conquered its way westward to Spain and eastward to India. But the Arabian Knights, the Holy War itself? They were in the service of Sinbad the Sailor.[17] The Arab world was therefore based on completely different foundations than the European early Middle Ages: on global merchants, a blossoming manufacturing sector, and a rich system of trade, not a semiwilderness of fortifications, insignificant towns, and monasteries. Not only did more light shine in the Arab world than in Frankistan,[18] its light was more alive than that of the later European cloister schools and the universities they spawned.

In addition, alongside trade and commerce, the book was part of everyday life. Uninterrupted by any great migration of peoples, the traditions of late antiquity were still richly present. They were kept most alive in Syria, in the absence of Byzantine rigidity and transcendent sternness; Iamblichus, the most fervent of the pagan Neoplatonists, was Syrian.[19] Syrian Christians had been active as doctors long before Muhammad's time and were, in the earliest era of Islam, the translators of Greek philosophy into Arabic. It is, furthermore, impossible to overlook how the Arab world was influenced by the Iranian reverence for light,[20] by the intellectual freedom that had long characterized feudal Persia. This was clearly expressed by the invitation extended by Sasanian emperor Chosroes I to the last Greek philosophers after Justinian had driven them out of Athens.[21] Even though intellectual freedom had declined there as well, Chosroes had earned his theological name (Anushirwan, or "The Immortal") as the suppresser of naturalist-communist sects. And although, until its Islamicization, a caste of priests ruled the new Persian Empire through arid superstition and dogmatic ritual like never before, it was still the case that the demystifying power of the old Iranian religion of light continued to exist, and the belief prevailed that man could best help the good spirit in its fight [483] with evil through active reason and social institutions. Bukhara in particular, near which Avicenna was born and which lay under Baghdad's jurisdiction, belonged to Khorezmian-Iranian culture, and since the eighth century, Baghdad itself, under the caliph al-Mansur,[22] represented the best example of the unification of Arabic and Iranian culture. Thus, it was a city in which one knew more than just the Qur'an; it blossomed as both the site of the highest civilization at that time and a place where worldly culture prevailed over obscurantist orthodoxy. The attitude of free-spirited reflection that arose there was then carried to the far West of the same culture: to Córdoba. Yet philosophy, as noted, is in no way an exotic greenhouse plant in Islamic soil, for the latter, indeed, has its own Greek-Syrian tradition. All this explains and encompasses the character of these most significant Islamic thinkers: they were doctors rather than monks, naturalists rather than theologians. In medieval Europe, philosophers with natural scientific inclinations were as rare as they were abnormal (Roger Bacon and Albertus Magnus are almost the only ones),[23] but among the Arabic Scholastics, the opposite was the case. Natural science outweighs theology in their writings, even when they are interpreting the suras of the Qur'an (as shown by Avicenna's *Almahad*, in which he denies the physical resurrection of the dead as proclaimed in sura 36). And *worldly* knowledge was the jewel with which the rulers of the Islamic East and West, the Abbasids of Baghdad as well as the Umayyads of Córdoba, liked to bedeck themselves. This means that the caliph was no pope. Only much later, with the decline of Arab society's mercantile foundations, did the obscurantist influence of orthodoxy begin. Until that point, alongside the almost-unimpeded use and development of "heathen" antiquity, there shone what Roger Bacon praised as being particular to Arabic science: it was a *"scientia experimentalis."*[24] Alexander von Humboldt even went so far as to say that the Arabs were the inventors of the considered and purposive experiment.[25] How clear it is, therefore, that this foundation in the nonclerical way of thinking among the great doctor-philosophers of the Islamic Middle Ages differs from that of [484] feudal-clerical Europe. This despite their common starting point in Aristotle and despite the impact of mysticism that remained powerfully present in the Orient, especially under of the influence of Neoplatonism.[26]

DIFFERENT RELATIONSHIP OF KNOWLEDGE TO FAITH

And so it is no surprise that the thinkers outlined here felt themselves to be above faith.[27] They, of course, make general acknowledgements of faith, yet these are always tempered by a specific caveat, by a caveat such as a man would have with relation to children's fare or, better yet, by a man searching for truth amid the glitz and glitter of impure thought. The founders of faith, Avicenna says, pronounced in their time what the philosophers later taught, but they did it in their own veiled manner. They did it with pictures and parables because the revelation had been for all and should, therefore, avail itself of a metaphorical language comprehensible to all. Had it been revealed in a different way, then it would have been in vain. By contrast, it is the business of philosophy to examine religion with the understanding of the more advanced members of society, to allow evidence to take precedence over faith. In this way, the faith in the Qur'an, as the word of God, was transformed into an entirely different faith in the power of human reason. The result was that the relationship to inherited religion became one of tension precisely because it limited, and hence was only marginally capable of contributing to, inquiry. In this sense, there is nothing left of revelation and irrationalism within religion, before which reason is compelled to capitulate agnostically. Rather, the discourse of images can be solved like a rebus, and the veil of its representation leaves no mystery. For Avicenna, and particularly for Averroës, the highest incarnation of the human spirit is not Muhammad but Aristotle; science as absolute cannot be expressed more clearly than this. The Christian Scholastics certainly praised Aristotle when, from 1200 on, [485] they named him *praecursor Christi*,[28] but can one imagine him described in a similar fashion by Islamic philosophers as a mere precursor of Muhammad? He is here in no way a precursor: Averroës saw Aristotle as the very embodiment of human reason, while the light of Muhammad remains in the realm of early education, of myths and parables. This faith-knowledge relationship is indeed completely different from that in Christian Scholasticism. In the latter, from Anselm of Canterbury to Thomas,[29] the revelation was in no way to be seen as a parable. Even in the earliest, most objectively heretical church philosophers, such as Scotus Eriugena,[30] where the Neoplatonist Arabic influence is powerful, the *vera ratio* is still subordinated to the *vera auctoritas*, and reason is seen merely as a tool—the *verae religionis regulas exprimere*—for expressing clearly what faith knows to be true.[31] Albertus Magnus and especially Thomas turned the Arabic faith-knowledge relationship on its head: not only is positive religion not the popular precursor to philosophy, but this, the natural light, is a possible precursor of the Revelation. As far as Thomas may have pushed the substantial harmonization of faith and knowledge, he was still not able to escape the real religious and, above all, genuinely Christian paradox that had confronted Paul as the Wisdom of the World,[32] which Tertullian had formulated as follows: "credo quia absurdum, quia impossibile," or "the gospel is true because it is absurd and it is impossible."[33] Even in Thomas, the greatest, the most committed Aristotelian in Christianity, faith was, in all its central tenets, beyond reason—if not exactly against it, then certainly above it. And precisely because faith is ultimately impenetrable to the light of natural knowledge, it has merit. The difference between this and Avicenna's equation of knowledge and light (particularly as the highest light, the ur-light) could not be greater.

In this context, Eastern reason admittedly went into an alliance not quite of this world. For it was, indeed, not the only force in these times that pulled away from the letter of the text, transforming it into a mere shell.³⁴ The *mystical* movements also often supported, in a strange way,³⁵ the distance of such thinkers [486] from the believers in scripture. In the Orient, much like later in Europe with the Albigensians and Meister Eckhart,³⁶ this found expression in a number of people's movements against nobility and church. These movements, particularly within the Iranian elite, formed a lasting defense against Arabic Islam; here it took on Neoplatonist traits. Aristotle himself was often viewed by Avicenna in a Neoplatonic and even Gnostic light.³⁷ This type of Syrian-Iranian influence is unmistakable in Baghdad's cultural circle, a group inherently alien to the Qur'an as well as to Islamic ritual practice. In Baghdad, and still more in Basra, there was a continuation of the old Iranian myth of light, which was itself one of the origins of mystical gnosis, of light's journey and homecoming. With his naturalism, Avicenna had no connection to religious orthodoxy but rather to the cosmological metaphysics of light and, here and there (even Homer occasionally sleeps),³⁸ even to its superstitions (albeit minus astrology, which he tellingly rejected in one of his writings).³⁹ He interacted with the Sufis, the Persian mystical sect that, without regard to the Qur'an and not mediated through the mosque, taught of the pouring back of the soul into the cosmic ur-light. He also had contact with the Brethren of Purity of Basra, a learned sect founded in 950, who, in an encyclopedia still available today, wrote in Neoplatonist terms of the light-origin of the world so as to thereby gain reciprocal knowledge of the return of the world and soul, a sort of travel guide to the ur-light.⁴⁰ This is all mysticism and, as such, not yet worldliness; as mentioned, this mysticism—a peculiar yet undeniable ally—stood side by side with naturalism in the struggle with the church and scriptural orthodoxy.⁴¹ Religion was certainly not rejected in a purely *transcendental* mysticism, as opium for the people; it was considered, rather, as too little opium, yet in *pantheistically* oriented mysticism, tendencies showed themselves that came close to an awakening, if not out of a trance, then out of a condition of religious servitude. With the Sufis, positive faith dissolves in the inner view of the All-One; the Sufi recognizes the nothingness of all religions and feels himself above them, [487] existing as they do only for the uninitiated, spiritually sublime. The same is true, mixed with a popularized Neoplatonism, for the Brethren of Purity of Basra: positive religions are only transitional phases, pedagogical steps to a "pneumatic" truth;[42] they are ultimately dimmers of the Light, lands of deception. So said the mystic Abu Sa'id, a friend of Avicenna's: "Until the madrasah and the minaret lie in ruin / The work of the dervish is not complete / Until belief becomes disbelief, and disbelief belief / A servant of Truth does not become a Muslim."[43] Goldziher points concretely to the extent that the Sufis overlap in such thoughts with Islamic free thinkers, who came to the same conclusions on the basis of other considerations.[44] And if a mystic stressed the consequences of uniting with the divine too fervently, we know he could very quickly find himself making the executioner's acquaintance. The skipping over of religion thus stands as close to its own sublation as the descent of man in God does to the descent of God in man.[45] Lessing's allegory of the three rings—which goes back, via Boccaccio,[46] to the Saracen-influenced court of Holy Roman Emperor Frederick II—as well as the formula created there, of *de tribus impostoribus*—the three imposters, Moses, Jesus, and Muhammad—and all this irreligious enlightenment has as its origin, besides the lion's share of naturalism, this most paradoxical element of unchurchly mysticism.[47] It is—in nonpantheistic, in *human-eschatological* guise—fully palpable in Joachim of Fiore, in his teachings of a coming Third Testament, superior to the outdated Old and New.[48] The last time this enthusiastic antichurch enmity appeared was in the mysticism of fourteenth-century Germany, among the Brothers of the Free Spirit,[49] so reminiscent of the Sufis, and in Meister Eckhart's deification of humanity, the deification of reason.

Certainly, so as not to exceed the aim of grounded truth, mysticism could be as hostile toward knowledge as it could be toward churches, and this was especially the case in reactionary times. Avicenna's work itself fell prey to this tendency as soon as mysticism aligned with orthodoxy [488] and persecuted philosophy.

This was introduced (characteristically combined with skepticism toward reason) by Al-Ghazali, who began as a professor of philosophy in Baghdad but wrote his highly influential *Destructio Philosophorum* against philosophy and in praise of mysticism and then spent his older years as a Sufi—only, however, in order to drive the pantheistic tradition out of mysticism and replace it with an orthodox-transcendental one.[50] "If the sun rises," said this renegade from philosophy, "one can do without Saturn," or in other words, without the planet of thought, of knowledge and science.[51] For him, the sun was the Qur'an, and Avicenna's main theories—the eternal nature of matter, the incorruptibility of the law of causality, the nonresurrection of the dead—were saturnine and accursed. However, alongside the sort of mysticism that led to and finally collapsed into obscurantism, there were also those who, in their way, supported Avicenna's subordination of the word to cognitive truth. As becomes clear in the end, though, the *whole doctrine of religion as an allegorical veil* stems, at least formally, from mysticism and not from pure enlightenment. Neoplatonism, following the Stoics and the pantheists, first drew all the ideas of religion in the known world (the Greek as well as the Oriental) into this allegorism, into the reinterpretation of religious allegories as philosophical concepts. The Christian patristic Origen gave us the theory of the threefold meaning of the biblical text: the somatic-literal, the psychic-allegorical, and the pneumatic-mystical.[52] Yet there can be no doubt that the "Truth" that the Neoplatonists, and then Origen, believed they had found was not the same as that which the Enlightenment, already in Avicenna, meant as a rational kernel. Mystical allegorism (often a wild-goose chase of arbitrary interpretations) occurred mainly in order to save religion, not to criticize it or reduce it, let alone to transcend it through wisdom.[53] In any case, it was always assumed in these exercises that the religious pronouncement and the insights of reason would have precisely the same content—an assumption that [489] Avicenna was in no way prepared to make. Despite this, his ideas on the relationship between faith and knowledge originated from Neoplatonist allegorism and, in rational form—in Avicenna's form—this relationship bore its fruit throughout the whole of the European Enlightenment.

ALIVE, SON OF AWAKE, GOD AS CELESTIAL BODY

The play of knowledge and faith has itself been handed down in allegories, not only in the fable of the three rings, but also in a widely printed book by Ibn Tufayl: *Alive, Son of Awake*, one of the first philosophical novels.[54] And his tale likewise went into the European canon, more widely known even than that of the three rings: Ibn Tufayl's novel served as a model not only for *Robinson Crusoe* but for all subsequent Robinsonesque tales. Yet the novel itself harks back conceptually to Avicenna, and the wakeful title comes quite literally from him. In order to demonstrate how completely adequate rational thought is, Avicenna invented a character who lived in complete isolation but nevertheless came to full intellectual cognition and had the characteristic antiopium name *Hayy ibn Yaqzan*, or *Alive, Son of Awake*.[55] The "Awake" is the active general intellect that fills and connects all people. And this is the reason that, one hundred years later in Arabian Spain, Averroës's teacher Ibn Tufayl wrote his philosophical novel of the same name, *Alive, Son of Awake*, in which Avicenna's fiction was to find its greatest test. Right on time for the early European Enlightenment, this novel appeared in 1671 under the title *Philosophus Autodidactus* and was translated into German in 1783 by Eichhorn as *Der Naturmensch*, a title suggesting, in Rousseauian fashion, the end of the early rationalist Enlightenment project.[56] The novel did not, however, merely call Robinson onto the stage but also reinforced the basic tenet of the Enlightenment, that faith is not necessary if one has reason, for Avicenna-Tufayl's *Philosophus Autodidactus* bears witness to the power of nature and wisdom unspoiled by the teachings of priests and without the mystical surrogates of those who never learned to think properly, [490] the mass of people who have been kept far from proper thought. Even so, the latter type ultimately achieves the highest level of knowledge of which their independent thinking is capable: the *unio mystica*.[57] Here, too, as in general, naturalism includes a healthy dose of mysticism alongside the traditions of an Islamic culture stuck in the Middle Ages. Yet, among the great thinkers, naturalism was not suspended; rather, especially in Avicenna's case and together with the greatest proponents of natural science, it maintained freedom from the Qur'an and from orthodoxy. Once enlightenment is abandoned, only a sort of ecstasy can function, and as a result, Ibn Tufayl's Crusoe—as the last stage of his education in reason—gets lost in God. How foreign to naturalism it is to see Ibn Tufayl praise Avicenna of all people—alongside the Sufis—as a master of this ecstasy. In support of this claim, he cites the following text from Avicenna:

> Then, when his training and willpower reach a certain point, glimmerings of the light of Truth will flicker before him, thrilling him like lightning, flashing and going out. If he is diligent in his ascetic practice, these spells grow more and more frequent, until they come unasked, entrancing him without the use of exercises. No matter what he looks at, he will turn from it to the Sacred Presence, reminded of some aspect of the Divine, and again he will be overwhelmed. Thus he begins to see the Truth in everything. Finally his efforts bring him to a stage where his moment of recognition turns to tranquil contemplation; his stolen glimpses, familiarity; his spark, a limpid flame. He has gained an understanding as unshakable as that of an old friendship, . . . his inmost being becomes a polished mirror facing toward the truth. Sublime delight pours over him, and he rejoices in his soul at all the marks it bears of Truth. He still hesitates between them; but then, becoming oblivious to self, he is aware only of the Sacred Presence—or if he is at all aware of himself, it is only as one who gazes on the Truth. At this point, communion is achieved.[58]

With this quotation, Ibn Tufayl refers to Avicenna's lost *Philosophia Orientalis*, which declares, however, that not only the Qur'an but

Aristotelian philosophy itself contains the truth, albeit hidden behind a veil. The [491] unveiled truth was only to be found in the *Philosophia Orientalis*, as a philosophy not of the Orientals but of the Orient, of the rising of the sun, of illumination. Averroës, in turn, maintained in *Destructio Destructionis* that Avicenna's *Philosophia Orientalis*—in full pantheistic mode—agreed with late-antique Aristotle commentator Alexander of Aphrodisias, according to whom,

> There must exist a spiritual force which is diffused in all the parts of the universe in the same way as there is a force in all the parts of a single animal which binds them together.... Many of Avicenna's followers ... ascribe this opinion to him.... This is the view which he has laid down in his *Oriental Philosophy*, and they say that he only called this book *Oriental Philosophy* because it is the doctrine of the Orientals; for they believed that according to the Orientals divinity is located in the heavenly bodies, as Avicenna himself had come to believe.[59]

Now, after all that, Avicenna's declared ecstasy appears neither quite so devoid of enlightenment nor so far from naturalism, for the saint, whose gate Avicenna's ecstatic has reached, does not live in a state of natureless transcendence but is Allah, as the inflowing of nature itself, at its highest level through the starry heavens above. At this point, mysticism, in which Avicenna–Ibn Tufayl's *Son of Awake* concludes, clearly becomes pantheistic once again. Aristotle, with a polytheistic accent, sees the stars as gods; in Avicenna, the godhead, with an accent of monist tension, suffuses the whole of nature; in this way, his ecstasy unites the abstracted soul and the starry heavens as the same abstracted nature. This is quite a departure from the movements on the earth (under the moon), but naturalism (God=*corpus coeleste*)[60] is preserved, along with wakefulness, in Avicenna's mysticism. What remains: faith, as a veiled parable, gave knowledge exactly the level of independence that could be achieved at that time. Knowledge, often coupled with ecstasy and the body, stayed true to nature; indeed, matter raised nature to the heavens. [492]

ARISTOTLE-AVICENNA AND THE ESSENCES OF THIS WORLD

We come closer now to Ibn Sina, although this is not the place for a detailed exposition.[61] That would bring with it many contemporary concerns unrelated to the possible inheritance discussed here and would thus be only historically and not philosophically noteworthy. As a living being, Avicenna had quite different concerns: thus, he has been described as a landmark within the authentically continued Aristotelian tradition as well as a landmark of the Enlightenment, beginning in the Middle Ages, of the beginnings of matter as a higher category, in the manner that Avicenna himself appeared to his native orthodoxy and to Christian Scholasticism.[62] Avicenna's division of philosophy is already less loyal to a theological schema than is that of the Christian [493] Aristotelians. After propaedeutic studies in logic and mathematics, Avicenna requires a broad spectrum of natural sciences and natural philosophy, and only afterward, built upon these, comes metaphysics. Yet this natural empiricism in its structure, so to speak, the main emphasis of the encyclopedia, is not the distinguishing mark of Avicenna's work. Rather, what is distinctive about it, what secures the coherence of his legacy and much more, is the line he emphasized leading from Aristotle, not to Thomas, but to Giordano Bruno and his successors. For this line and its direction, I propose here, corresponding to the well-known fork in thought after Hegel's death, the description *Aristotelian Left*.[63] There is a similarity between the naturalistic ways in which the Aristotelian *nous* and the Hegelian Spirit were brought down to earth. This similarity should certainly not be exaggerated: Aristotle is not Hegel, the social causes underlying the divergence of their respective intellectual descendants are quite different, the periods of time before the advents of their respective Lefts differ, and between Avicenna here and the Hegelian Left there, there is a difference in format. Nonetheless, there are correspondences: in both cases there is an increasingly predominant interest in the worldly; in the case of Avicenna, the integration of Aristotelian *nous* into a stronger naturalism; in the case of the Hegelian Spirit, a naturalism that radically changes everything. And with regard to the time it took for both Aristotle and Hegel to become naturalized, a Left Wing also emerged, almost immediately in Aristotle's case. Aristotle had defined matter as "dynamei-on," merely what-may-become-possible,[64] as indeterminate in itself, and which, like wax, passively takes on and can be molded by any form. The form (the cause of the goal, the shape of the goal, entelechy) is thus the only actively effective thing;[65] and the highest form, the *actus purus* completely free of matter,[66] is the *nous*, the pure God of thought. And yet this very doctrine received its first left-wing interpretation from as local a source and as quickly as Hegel's, for Strato, the third leader of the peripatetic school,[67] already weakened the theism of pure *nous* and considerably separated it from matter. Strato, with the sobriquet "the Physicist," gave Aristotelianism its first naturalistic twist. He was followed by the [494] aforementioned great late-antique Aristotle commentator Alexander of Aphrodisias, who initiated the concept of the highest potency of matter, which, as we shall see, led Avicenna to provide matter to active form and, by the same token, provide active form to matter. It is this naturalization that begins with Avicenna and which is then advanced by the Jewish Andalusian philosopher Avicebron in the concept of *materia universalis*,[68] and by Averroës, in whose writings matter becomes something eternally in flux and alive in the form of "natura naturans," in no need of a God-*nous* from above or beyond.[69] This tradition continued in the Renaissance, when Giordano Bruno (a devotee of Avicebron and Averroës)[70] shifted from a theistic position to one—albeit still pantheistic—which saw matter as a *fructifying and fecund universal life*,[71] infinite like God had been, yet without a beyond. This line, derived from the Aristotelian matter-form concept, and its effect, namely *the sublation of divine potency itself in the active potentiality of matter*,[72] is the primary path of the Aristotelian Left, with Avicenna as its postantiquity landmark and turning point. By contrast, the Aristotelian Right, leading to Thomas, elevated the concept of *nous* even further than Aristotle already had. This Right relegated matter to mere potentiality, that is, totally incapable of effectuating itself in the world out of bare "dynameion," "what-may-become-possible."[73] To turn now to the issue of the Left in Avicenna; there are *three main points* in which Aristotle is developed naturalistically. These are, *first*, the doctrine of *body and soul*; *second*, that of *active understanding* or *universal human intelligence*; and *third*, the *relationship between matter and form (potentiality-potency)* in the world. The first two of these points are intimately bound up with the third, with the left turn in the problem of matter and with its elevation in importance.

1. With regard to *body and soul*, our thinker believes in the latter. Yet the soul is also present as desiring, feeling, and imagining in all animals and is therefore closely bound to the body. Soul exists only in and through the organic body as its unitary and indivisible active form. [495] In the human soul, however, the animalistic drive, fully shared with all animals, is complemented by understanding. This ensures not only that each human has its own soul—in contradistinction to the collective animal soul—but that this individual soul is also a lasting and indestructible one. This individual soul can be neither created by the body nor destroyed by its death. With this view, Avicenna does not yet distance himself from the Qur'an and Averroës, who is more consistent when he maintains that individual human souls, precisely because they are individual, end with death. Yet, insofar as Avicenna all the more decisively denied the resurrection of the *body*, he robbed the individual soul's immortality of all color. The absence of the body removes from the ruling church the sensory terror of hell, that enormous clerical stick,[74] and also removes the similarly sensory, hallucinogenic joy of heaven, that orthodox carrot. There is no such withdrawal of the body in medieval Christian thinkers, despite their common starting point with Avicenna and Averroës

in Aristotle's doctrine of the soul. In the Christian afterlife, terror burned brightly, and the dead marched their bodies through the fires of hell in order to feel their sins. For Avicenna, this feeling, belonging as it does to our animal soul, does not live on; the knowledge of this truth liberated at least those who held it from fear of eternal torture. What the conscious part of the soul that survived death was to experience, be it pure spiritual misery or happiness, was no longer available for clerical authority. It is no wonder that the ruling church persecuted such destroyers with their stick from the hereafter.

2. With regard to *individual understanding and universal reason*, Avicenna gives clear priority to the latter.[75] Here he has no hesitation and goes far beyond the narrow confines of individual uniqueness, custom, and faith. In Aristotle, individual understanding is described as the passive expression and *habitus* of the body to which it belongs.[76] It is passive because it is tied to the body and thus particularly close to the merely passive, receptive, and (at best) predisposed qualities of matter. By contrast, universal [496] reason is the active or authentic form, the effective power of the understanding; in this way, it becomes the impersonal center of the human being, independent of the habitus of the individual body. Aristotle's passive *nous* is simply that which is capable of cognition and which actively furnishes cognition. Yet, in Aristotle, there is no discussion of the relationship between this active reason and a human unity of reason. Such a unity was far from the mind of Aristotle, who saw slaves as speaking tools who only appeared to have the souls and the bodies of free persons; indeed, Aristotle saw all non-Greeks as natural slaves. He did not even think that active reason was common to all Greeks but that it remained an element of divine spirit. The nonindividuated nature of active reason in Avicenna and Averroës accordingly appears to be entirely different. In their work, active reason is defined first and foremost as the site of the *unity of human intellect*. From being the mere expression of the nonhabitual, the nonindividual, active reason becomes a human universal. Its content, however, is not

religion—and least of all any particular named confession—but rather philosophy, and Aristotelian philosophy in particular. By the same token, this is not to be seen as an individual or, indeed, confessional philosophy but comes about, as Averroës says, simply because Aristotle embodies the "highest human perfection, the final aim of human intellect."[77] Admittedly, the ways in which universal reason emerges in humans become fantastical constructs in Islamic thinkers, and especially in Avicenna. According to him, active intellect caps off the series of supernatural intelligences that flow down from God via the spirits of the planets to the "mover of the moon."[78] From there, active intellect flows directly into our understanding, illuminates it, and creates in it an image of the cosmic essences. This is Neoplatonist emanation theory, and indeed, in a form (with its ten dependent intelligences or spirits of the spheres) in which it shortly afterward is reproduced in the Kabbalah.[79] This [497] arch-mythical and astral-mythical position is far removed from naturalism. And yet, in Avicenna, active intellect, even as the "lowest level of heavenly intelligence,"[80] is not astral in its effect, nor does it, as it threatens to in Aristotle, shoot astray and end up in the divine spirit. Instead, it is the unity of human beings that sprouts out from it, as does the tolerance taught through the doctrine of the *unitas intellectus*: there is only one single Reason among humans, and this Reason is the same in all people. Regardless of how much the Stoics emphasized this unitas intellectus by dint of the doctrine of basic conceptions common to all people,[81] it was still Avicenna who gave this idea the sharp edge that cut through all prevailing confessional orthodoxy. With their simple idea of the leveling down of all people, the Stoics merely reflected the melting pot of the Roman Empire and were, in this way, no threat to the ruling class. On the other hand, the way that Avicenna, and after him Averroës, used the idea of the unitas intellectus also cut deeply into the arrogance of the religion of their own lands, the faith of Islam, whose adherents believed that beyond its boundaries lay only the darkness of night. The unity of active reason in all human beings was just as harmful to the absolute values of Christianity, represented by Saint Peter's power of the keys.[82] It is no wonder, therefore, that the clergy of both religions attacked such damaging ideas as grave heresy; in the West also, the doctrine of the unitas intellectus, in the shape given to it by Avicenna and Averroës, was mainly condemned as heresy. In order not to be confused with this Aristotelian Left, both Albertus Magnus and Thomas Aquinas wrote "De Unitate Intellectus contra Averroistas,"[83] for the watchword is clear: in Avicenna's unity of reason there appears nothing less than a new *pathos of tolerance*. This did not mean that a philosopher had to suffer what was downright false and palpably bad, but it represented an opposition to clericalism, to ignorance and the aggression of nostalgiacs who turned to zealotry out of egotism and stupidity. Tolerance and human reason rose above all this and rallied its supporters—as a majority. For the revolutionary Baptists, who were in no way blindly tolerant, the unitas intellectus became the Pentecostal Spirit of [498] Poor Conrad everywhere in the world;[84] "high above the scattering of all peoples and their faiths," as Thomas Münzer preached.[85] When the Enlightenment came, with its multifaceted value concept of "nature," Avicenna's unitas intellectus was at work alongside other traditions. The unity of universal reason can be found, only half-hidden by neo-Stoicism, precisely in the Enlightenment's overarching ideas of natural law, natural morality, and natural religion. Thus, there is peace within the interpretive framework of *intellectus agens vel universalis*,[86] which means this: peace to all who are of this right and active knowledge.

3. With regard to the *matter-form relationship*, our thinker also increasingly reshaped it. He was not the first to do so, but only after Avicenna, and through him, can we discern a recognizable school. As we have seen, Strato, one of Aristotle's successors, remained alone in his views on the incorporation of the active form into matter. This is because actual philosophical work within the peripatetic school was close to dying out; it had become specialized within individual branches of knowledge and hence scattered. Only the redoubtable Alexander of Aphrodisias, noted earlier,

further developed Stratonism, with its thoroughly naturalistic teachings. Even though he taught of a *soma theion*, God as a heavenly body, he also revived what Cicero passed down as Strato's central doctrine: "omnem vim divinam in natura sitam esse," all divine power is to be found in nature, with no need for a transcendental God. Yet the Aristotelian Left of the Middle Ages did not emerge out of the teachings of Strato or the commentator Alexander but from Avicenna's work on that point of points, on the concept of matter. And it was only Avicenna's *Philosophia Orientalis* that made Averroës aware of Alexander of Aphrodisias's protopantheism. Now Aristotle himself—this is a central point to reiterate in considering the impact of the Left Wing—had taught that matter was in the first place something completely indeterminate and unformed, out of which, itself uncreated, all things can be created. This prime matter, or ur-matter, still completely separate from the acting form, is only passive potentiality and therefore exists only incompletely. By contrast, [499] if matter is already bound up with active forms—as it is in all its worldly manifestations—then the enduring potential of "dynamei-on," "what-may-become-possible,"[87] is complemented by something of a collaborative sort. This collaboration individuates and determines the appearance and imprint of active form, often also in the sense of a disturbance. This second matter,[88] or matter that has come to the world, matter that includes its purposively shaping active forms or entelechies, can only be realized as "kata to dynaton," corresponding to "what-is-considered-possible."[89] In Aristotle, however, matter always remains essentially "dynamei-on," passive "what-may-become-possible," potentiality (even if, in the world's shaped matter, as something negatively participatory depending on the case, as a sine qua non).[90] For Aristotle, the only self-realizing active form is potency, an act within an event, and this all the way up to the fully immaterial act of the unmoved mover, God. Even in this case, however, movement is not inherent in matter, although it does represent the transition from a condition of possibility into one of actuality. Rather, Aristotle sees movement as part of entelechy, and he calls it an "unfinished entelechy."[91] It is evident that Aristotle's concept of matter is imbued with the character of *objective possibility* but not, or at least not yet, with the distinguishing characteristics of ferment and pregnancy, of self-creation, of the sheer incompleteness of this possibility. There are undoubtedly hints of this notion of possibility, for example, in the law of "hormē," the drive of matter toward form (which represents, as it were, the objective being, the material being of Platonic Eros). Despite this strong hint of a process-agent within matter itself, Aristotle never overcame the equation of matter with passivity. As a result, the privilege bestowed upon immaterially conceived entelechy as the effective agent remained unshaken, just like the notion of matter being imprinted with form that animates and develops itself.

Avicenna, to be sure, followed these Aristotelian teachings; he kept matter and active form separate, but he did so in a way that made matter ever more important. The active form, especially in its highest, divine manifestation, hence becomes the mere dot on the material *i* [500] or the mere exhalation that releases material forms. And, indeed, in Avicenna, in his tracts in *Metaphysika*, from his philosophical encyclopedia, this is expressed in the following way: the type of possibility that precedes reality presupposes a subject that contains within it the possibility of its own emergence.[92] This subject is matter, which, as a precondition for its emergence, cannot itself have emerged and therefore has to be both primordial and eternal. With this step, and in a surprising manner, Avicenna logically sharpens the Aristotelian doctrine of uncreated matter, precisely from within the concept of possibility. Matter is, therefore, an eternal essence, like form, and in no way a simple being that has done away with its own Being; rather, it is, with regard to form, the substrate of its predispositions, and indeed, already including its specific manifestations. Avicenna goes on to maintain that in addition to the subject of possibility, there must be a causal subject of realization, for whatever gives reality to possibility cannot simply be possibility itself. Consequently, just as matter must be presupposed as the possibility of anything's existence, there must be assumed to be a nonimmanent cause, a *dator formarum*, or form giver, which raises things from possibility to actuality. Immediately, however, Avicenna limits this efficacy of a divine cause to the mere creation and preservation of existence. Within this *actus purus*, therefore, there is no content (no Whatness, essence)[93] *that is not already predisposed within the objective possibility of matter, indeed, that is not preformed*; and God alone can awaken matter. God, or Aristotle's immaterial actus purus, thus becomes the fiat within form,[94] such that the form giver becomes the giver of a signal for the emergence of that which was already prepared for development, and therefore the sum total of the essences, the Whatnesses, the substances of the forms, does not rest within God. It may well be that the abstract *materia prima* in itself cannot by any stretch contain the multitude, let alone the sum of all forms, but it is certainly the case that they exist within the *concrete material of the world* that has come about as a result of the past mixing of forms [501]: "The things that specify matter are the things that prepare it. The preparer is that through which there comes to be, in the thing prepared, something by virtue of which its appropriateness for [the reception] of a specific thing is more appropriate than [the reception of] some other thing. . . . This is nothing other than the complete appropriateness for a specific thing—namely, that for which it is prepared."[95] The essences themselves exist already as specific material predispositions, so specific that Avicenna holds them to be educed in three ways in accordance with the number of types of motion in Aristotelian physics.[96] There are three types: change in location, change in quality, organic metamorphosis—each category contains a specific form that corresponds to a specifically determined material possibility. Thus, the concept of a separate form must dissolve and, at least with Avicenna, although not at first with Averroës, transfer some of its Active-Actuality into matter.[97] Indeed, Avicenna, in his doctrine of the elements, calls form the "immanent fire" or the "fiery truth" of matter.[98] It is not a big leap from this restructuring of the matter-form relationship to the immanence of design or natura naturans in Averroës. According to Averroës, matter does not only carry within it all forms as the kernels of life but also the movement essential to matter and not, as in Aristotle, entelechy. According to Averroës, it is "the circular motion of the heavens" that allows the forms, which have been waiting for eternity within matter, to emerge.[99] For this reason, Averroës says in the decisive sentence from his *Destructio Destructionis*: "Generatio nihil aliud est nisi converti res ab eo, quod es potential ad actum," the generation of a thing is nothing but the transformation of its potentiality into the actuality that already existed within it.[100] And the forms it takes emerge only from the matter itself—development is *"eductio formarum ex materia."* Thus, the orientation of the Aristotelian Left emerges via the reconstruction of the matter-form relationship as one that clearly grasps matter as an active force—not just as something mechanically inert. In place of a God who created the world there stands the creative power of natura naturans—toward [502] natura naturata. It even should not have been so difficult to push forward, via the concept of development, to the problem of a natura-supernaturans and accordingly to a natura-supernaturata.[101] Both would have placed heaven, that is, as a no-longer-free-floating spiritual form projected into the future, on its possible feet. *Yet the "eductio formarum ex materia" was enough, as both a test tube and a latent treasury, to lay hold of a new concept of matter.* It is also, then, no wonder that here, too, the Islamic orthodoxy condemned Avicenna and Averroës and burned both their effigies in the form of their works, just as the Christian Inquisition later burned Giordano Bruno in the flesh.

AVICENNA'S INFLUENCE ON AQUINAS, AND WHAT AQUINAS REJECTED

Nothing would be more false than to simply play off the Left, detailed here, against the Christian monastic thinkers. The days of undervaluing European Scholasticism have long passed, and whenever such disdain now occasionally shows itself, it appears foolish.

Moreover, Christian Scholasticism is so diverse that one cannot call it an Aristotelian Right in the same way that one can identify a Left within the Islamic tradition. Furthermore, the classical Christian Scholasticism represented by Albert and Thomas is of one mind with Avicenna on many points. This is particularly the case in epistemology, as per Avicenna's extraordinary distinction between a *first* cognitive intention, directed toward objects, and a *second* one, directed toward the mere concepts of those objects.[102] Avicenna's conclusions about the *problem of universals*, that is, about the real validity of general concepts, were taken up wholesale by Albert and Thomas. Universals or general concepts accordingly have validity ante rem with regard to the world's plan, in re with regard to nature, post rem with regard to abstracting cognition. Here, and two hundred years in advance, Avicenna formulated the solution that was later reckoned among the Albertan-Thomistic heights of Christian Scholasticism. On [503] this point, Albertus Magnus and Thomas often presented Avicenna as an authority, although on this point, Christian Scholasticism is no more on the Right than Avicenna is on the Left. Indeed, with regard to the later inroads made by the reduction of universals to the mere post rem of human cognition, in Ockham's nominalism,[103] one finds even more of a Left than was ever possible in the times of Avicenna and Averroës, namely, the beginnings of the bourgeois turn toward the worldly. Christian Scholasticism should, therefore, not be simply or generally characterized in any way as part of the Aristotelian Right, at least not in terms of logical and epistemological questions. Nonetheless, on the whole, a few decisive points are certain: the clerical foundation, along with the corresponding of nonnaturalistic apologetics of the High Middle Ages, permits us, with the already-noted exceptions, to speak of an *Aristotelian Right*. The Catholic systems of the High Middle Ages took Aristotle not only as praecursor Christi but also more decisively as precursor of feudal-clerical class society and its ideology. Thomas posits a wide divide between body and soul, which in Aristotle is in no way clear, between *formae inhaerentes* of the world, trapped in matter, and the immaterial *formae separatae* of the supernatural world,[104] with the pure divine Spirit-Form at its apex. One can also compare the natura naturans, the heartbeat of matter in Averroës, with the following definition from Aquinas: "Oportet quod premum materiale sit maxime in potentia et ita (!) maxime imperfectum,"[105] or "matter is the richest of possibilities and therefore the most incomplete."[106] Here one hears precisely the inverted tones of the matter-form relationship found in Avicenna and Averroës, and it is far away, indeed, from the inclusion of all forms in a self-generating matter. If Oriental thinkers first reduced the importance of Aristotle's separation of the forms on high from matter and then abolished it altogether, Aquinas dualizes the *formae separatae* and *formae inhaerentes* to a degree far beyond Aristotle. And it is here that Thomas posits a fully transcendental theism of pure [504] spirit, where the Aristotelian Left introduced the concept of the explication of the world out of itself. By contrast, the positing and explication of the world out of the ultimately transcendent characterizes the powerful tradition of Right Aristotelianism in High Christian Scholasticism. A fresco from the workshop of Giotto in Santa Maria Novella in Florence shows Averroës—alongside the heretics Arius and Sabellius—thrown down at the feet of Aquinas, completely "refuted."[107] High Christian Scholasticism would, indeed, otherwise not be the entelechy of feudal-clerical society, with its pathos of hierarchy, which extends from its foundation up into the concept of the world and the heavens like a cathedral. Instead of the self-realization of many world-forms in matter itself, the pure active form rules on high, and its annex, the world, is at best a vassal. The productive element in this product severs it from the above; its agent also sits enthroned where it informs humans and the earth. Thomas's system was a brilliantly rigorous attempt to balance Aristotle, the Bible, dogma (about which Augustine was less concerned), yet the power of Avicenna's matter, not to mention Averroës's natura naturans, fit in this rigorous *Summa* as contrarily and uncomfortably as Goethe's Earth Spirit,[108] chained as it was to the clattering weaving looms of the epoch, fit in a church.

And yet, all this notwithstanding, the young Thomas also had to contend with Arabic influences. The manifest delight he took in sensory data meant that this master did not simply fall from heaven. Paris, where he began his teaching career, was influenced by the Averroism of Siger of Brabant,[109] according to whom knowledge, precisely as knowledge, did not need to end up in inherited faith. One of the Aristotelian doctrines was that the rational soul common to all humans was One; this meant that the posthumous survival of individual consciousness ceased to apply. Thomas even wrote a work against this heresy (*De unitate intellectus contra Averroistas*) in which he sought to combat the influence of Siger's interpretation of the unity of intellect, yet the fight against this "confusion" shows only that there was something here to be confused about. Above all, Aquinas explained throughout the whole of his life that the creation of the world at the beginning of time could not be proved philosophically; in this case, he was in agreement with the Jewish Aristotelian Maimonides,[110] who [505] likewise came out of Averroist cultural circles. As it is, Aristotle's original works already provided enough fodder for ruptures between his immanent explanation of the world and the church's transcendental explanation. Yet, here, too, Aquinas ultimately took a harmonizing position in the middle, with *suum quique* and hidden contradictions under the scepter of a church that was at first mistrustful but which soon began itself to search for a middle way.[111] In this manner, already to the young Aquinas (although his heresies were not yet known to all or even clear), Aristotle had become invariably transcendental—as per the "correct" way of reading him—and thus relativized. Since that time, the church has accordingly held the following proposition to be valid: Aristotelian philosophy is the epitome of truths collectively accessible through *lumen naturale*,[112] truths that are not contradicted by revelation, but which are reshaped and complemented by it. As a result, the Latin Averroists, who detached philosophy from its theological leads, disappeared completely from official Scholasticism and, a bit later, also from nominalistic late Scholasticism. Indeed, as a result, the very issue that the contemporary Scholastic Alexander of Hales (independent of Averroism) still identified as the *most important* lost its significance in Thomas's work—or at least stopped being a central concern: namely, the *immanent* upheaval and sufficiency of *act* and *potentiality, form* and *matter*.[113] Instead, Thomas placed the transcendental ur-act of God at the center of the cosmos and transformed it from something that, in Aristotle, was only the *final cause* of the world and its creations into something that was the *efficient* cause of the world as such, with the powers of creation and of conferring being absolute.[114] Accordingly, Aquinas ultimately removes that which realizes forms itself (entelechy) and relegates this act to an *exclusive gift* of the *divine* Act-Being, the Being of realization, subordinating it to the totally transcendental. In this, Aquinas surprisingly seems to follow the Arabic additions to Aristotle; namely, the particularly sharp separation we find first in Avicenna between Essence and Being, *essentia* and *existentia*.[115] Avicenna, following the Neoplatonic model, had, in fact, distinguished the contingent existence of things in the world from a necessary divine Being [506] out of which the former flowed, emanated. Yet, for Avicenna, and even more so for Averroës, the effective Act-Being of worldly entelechies remained thoroughly *self-creating*, in its potentiality-potency matter, while for Aquinas, however, the world—only ever a creation, never creative—largely withdraws, and the Act-Being finally assumes the role of the worldly entelechies.[116] The thing that "natures," the creative power of a natura naturans,[117] thereby becomes as meaningless and unreal as an entelechy, taken as impressed form, that is nonetheless capable, alive and self-activating, of developing itself. Even if the creative capacity of realization is not completely eliminated, in Thomas it is only considered as a gift from above and never without the participation of that unique power of Being, the transcendental power of God. Only this total Real,[118] no longer restricted by potentiality or unrealized possibilities, can have any real effect, that is, can lead from possibility to reality.[119] Thus a total Real—*not to be confused in any way with an incomplete and fermenting natura naturans*—can only be found in that God or fixed transcendent thing of which Aquinas says, "The essence of God is nothing other than his being,"[120] or—in a translation of "I will be what I will be" (Exodus 3:14), albeit devoid of any future dimensions—"I am He who Is. That is the proper name for God."[121] This contention that God's essence alone contains within it all existence should not be understood in the sense of the ontological argument for the existence of God (Ens perfectissimum eo ipso = Ens realissimum),[122] an argument that Thomas, who is in no way aprioristic, subordinates to the so-called cosmological argument for the existence of God (inferring a final cause of being from His works).[123] And, indeed, matter itself also plays a role in Aquinas: it is the *principium individuationis*; it thus determines the *plurality* of individual examples of a species form (according to which there are individual humans and not only *humanitas* and various heavenly bodies [507] rather than just *stellaritas*).[124] Indeed, the entelechy-vassals have only been *gifted* their actions, and accordingly, the *sole causality* of God has no place here (as was claimed in the Arab world outside of and against Avicenna and Averroës, in the reactionary sectarian philosophy of the *mutakallim*).[125] Not only did the loosening of the bonds [between being and matter], the fundamental relocation of the determining factor in existence into the heavens above, damage Aristotelian immanence itself; even more so, it left no place—literally *au fond*—for a Left-Aristotelian concept of matter with *its own logos spermatikos*.[126] Consequently, any emancipatory *natura naturans* from below (self-creating matter)[127] could only ever appear to the Aristotelianism of the church, clear as the light of day, as the work of sulfurous Lucifer. Bruno would feel its wrath, and for those who followed transcendent orthodoxy, Spinoza carried its *signum reprobationis*, its "mark of depravity," on his brow precisely because of his doctrine of *natura sive deus*. The transcendentally relocated energeia of Aristotle's entelechies took with it Faust's "seeds and effective power,"[128] removing them most decisively from the world (and with them the development of the world out of itself) and transferring them to the heavens, the only place from which matter could be created and guided according to the absolutism from above, which alone confers worth and being.

THE ARISTOTELIAN LEFT'S INFLUENCE ON THE ANTICHURCH

It is time to acknowledge the residual effects of the given Left more consciously than heretofore. They emerged long before the bourgeois morning, in surprising form indeed. In literature, there is the *Romance of the Rose*, from the thirteenth century,[129] thoroughly embracing the world, full of the disengagement of the flesh from the spirit yet also full of the ensoulment of worldly matter. It was not a heavenly rose for which the garden of this novel was constructed; here the world of love lives as love of the world, and Averroës was its godfather. Besides such sanguine free thought, there is also the academic scandal of a Christian–anti-Christian Averroism, beginning at the Sorbonne, reproduced until the [508] Renaissance and the Baroque at the University of Padua. The main issues here were not only the denial of individual immortality and its equally controversial surrogate in the persistence of universal reason. Rather, the problem of matter stood at its center, the priority of the material *substantia orbis*, as in Averroës's homily of the same name.[130] In particular, the jurist John of Jandun and, later and less strongly, the physician Pietro d'Abano had both, in their capacities as philosophers,[131] defended the preexistence of matter against the church and its teachings about Creation. Since the world already potentially existed before it became actual (stepped into reality), it is just as eternal as the substrate of its possibility, matter. All this, however, takes a back seat to the repercussion felt not only in elegant poetry or in the shadows of the lecture hall.

The burning aftermath of the new matter-form relationship showed itself elsewhere, in dangerous sects and in martyrs. As for the sect leaders, around 1200, [it appeared] in the pantheistic heretics Amalric of Bena and David of Dinant.[132] They were the heads of the sect of the Amalricians and stood out among those whom the church who were deemed zealots by dint of the "matter" of their spirit. A relationship to the Albigensian movement is not absent here, and the same goes for Joachim of Fiore, who simultaneously announced the political arrival of the free Holy Spirit. Yet the Holy Spirit in David of Dinant brought something curious; it came considerably more from Baghdad and Córdoba, from Avicenna and Averroës, than from heaven. Albertus Magnus reports that David taught, "Deus, hyle et mens una sola substantia sunt," God, matter, and spirit are of one single substance, to which Thomas adds, "Stultissime posuit deum esse materiam primam."[133] Insofar as God, matter, and spirit are substantially the same and God is nothing other than prime matter out of which everything came to be and in which all forms are contained, form also lost out to matter in the West.[134] For a long time, David of Dinant, of course, remained without followers—the stake exterminated them; this doctrine came into contact with the Renaissance too early and first becomes visible in Giordano Bruno. Its contact with the past is also palpable [509] in Avicebron,[135] the Spanish Jewish philosopher between Avicenna and Averroës who had already united David of Dinant and Bruno before either existed. Avicebron, in the eleventh century, is the same person as the religious hymnist Solomon Ibn Gabirol, who was long assumed to be an Arab and is cited by Bruno as such, with almost greater reverence than [he cited] Avicenna and Averroës. His work *Fons Vitae* had little influence in Jewish Arabic cultural circles, but it was all the more influential in Christian and heretical ones. Indeed, it could be said: the Aristotelian Left, rising with Avicenna, joins in Avicebron with a most remarkable type of Neoplatonist Left in a manner that radically extended Plotinus's inherently mystical concept of "intelligible matter," high above by God, to a materia universalis within all the world's layers. To be sure, that extension was already purported in Avicenna's *Philosophia Orientalis*, and hence, it, along with Averroës's work, influenced David of Dinant and his successors. Yet Avicebron, more pointedly than Avicenna, conceives of his connecting materia universalis (reason as well as the body) as the substrate of the world's unified nexus of life. From a stone to the highest reason of the human species, "universal intelligence," everything is furnished by a single matter that ranges over all forms and from which only

God's will remains free. "I have now understood," says the student in the second treatise of *Fons Vitae*, "that particular natural matter subsists in universal natural matter, and universal natural matter subsists in universal heavenly matter, and universal heavenly matter subsists in universal corporeal matter, and universal corporeal matter subsists in universal spiritual matter."[136] There are thus supposed to be four higher forms of matter above particular natural matter that support the unity of the world; all are of the same substance without exception. This message of Eastern naturalism undoubtedly reached the pantheistic heretics of Europe, the message of matter as the substance of unity everywhere; David's formula, "Omnia in materia idem,"[137] suggests as much.

And now to Bruno, after whom matter's esteem finally begins to shine. The primacy of form disappears completely, and anything that supposedly prods or radiates from the [510] beyond is treated most scornfully. Instead, this self-fructifying, self-explicating matter, the forms of which develop toward the All, is autarchic. The artist of the world's development lives only in this natura naturans,[138] and the eternal God-Nature weaves alone for itself the eternal garment of the world, natura naturata. The perpetual drawing out of the richness of forms contained within matter is the cause of the world as we perceive it. Nowhere in Bruno, therefore, does matter remain passive, without act, without ability and perfection, "senzo atto, senza virtù e perfezione."[139] Bruno's glowing naturalism, which brings Avicenna, Avicebron, and Averroës fully to the world, is so capacious that he even views the Aristotelian concept of the drive of matter toward form (as something molding its shape) as being inconsistent with the autarchy of matter (as an eternal womb of creation).

> [Matter] does not desire those forms which daily change on its back.... There is as little reason to say that matter desires form as that it hates it.... By the same line of reasoning, according to which it is said to desire what it sometimes receives or produces, it can also be said to abhor whatever it throws off or rejects. In fact, it detests more fervidly than it desires, for it eternally throws off that

individual form after retaining it a very short while. The source of the forms cannot desire what is already within it, for one does not desire what one already possesses.[140]

And the intellectual affinity of Giordano Bruno to the Aristotelian Left, how it appears after so many centuries in this materialism of vitality, is furthermore a conscious one:

> This is why we find philosophers who, having pondered thoroughly the essence of natural forms, such as one may see in Aristotle and his kind, have finally concluded that they are only accidents and particularities of matter, so that, according to them, it is to matter that we must accord the privilege of being act and perfection, and not to the things of which we can truly say that they are neither substance nor nature, but relative to the substance and nature—that is to say, in their opinion, [511] matter, which for them is a necessary, eternal and divine principle, as it is to Avicebron, the Moor, who calls it "God who is in everything."[141]

Admittedly, Bruno himself does not entirely accept this complete displacement of the formal principle; Teofilo, the philosopher's representative, adds immediately afterward in the same dialogue that alongside the material principle, there indeed still exists a formal one, albeit closely associated with matter, and which he calls world-power, universal form. The material omnipotence is not thereby sublated,[142] however, as the formal principle of the world-soul is, for matter, only the "helmsman of the ship." And it is exactly this formal principle, which, as the highest, as God's will, "to Avicebron, the Moor," had contained no matter, is in Bruno, the thinker of total immanence, barely distinguishable from the glow of matter. Although Bruno called matter the first principle of being, and form its second principle, for him, matter is nonetheless the mother of all forms; the latter are its children, and there is no real difference in substance between matter-form. For this reason, Hegel is correct when he says about Bruno's principle, "Matter is nothing without efficacy; form is the power and the inner life of matter."[143] With this, Bruno makes Avicennian naturalism consistent: God is now not an independent factor in matter, but instead, matter itself incorporates the idea of the unmoved mover as the highest and most active expression of its own life. Only Spinoza's pantheism exhibits a more seamless intertwining of immanence, such that he no longer finds it necessary to refer terminologically or substantially to the matter-form relationship of Aristotle and his Left. Yet Spinoza also strays so little from the spirit of the aforementioned orientation that there are nonetheless substantial echoes of David of Dinant—who was almost certainly unknown to him—in Spinoza's unity of substance-attribute. "Deus hyle et mens una sola substantia sunt," David of Dinant had taught; this is unmistakably what Spinoza aims at with his real unity:[144] Deus sive natura et res extensa et res cogitans. The impartations of the Aristotelian Left thus reach far into the newer, world-immanent philosophy; intertwining East and West, a truth of materialism works [512] itself out. Lastly, it should be noted that something of a relationship exists, without pantheism, between Avicenna, Averroës, and the Leibnizian doctrine of immanent development.[145] Although in Leibniz, the matter-form problem is also terminologically submerged, the affinity between self-developing germ matter and the evolutionary series of sleeping, dreaming, awake monads is unmistakable. Indeed, on this point, Leibniz takes Averroism more genetically than Bruno does, making it the principle of the world's growing self-production.

RELIGION BROUGHT TO MORALITY

Even if books cannot make one good, they can nonetheless make one better or worse. Thus says Jean Paul,[146] and books that break new ground are no exception to this rule. Avicenna's books made yesterday's minds considerably worse; the same goes for Averroës's writings. For, as so often happens in history, the major concerns that arose in an environment suffused by torpor or only interested in intellectual torpor merely reflected its own limitations, multiplied and reinforced. This [happened] especially where a society, such as the Arab one, declined and began to rigidify, and a feudal-clerical damper laid itself atop what had earlier been a briskly moving, enterprising existence. This was soon the case in Arab culture—before the West knew its restorations and inquisitions. Islamic orthodoxy took vengeance on those who sublated faith into knowledge; they themselves were sublated. Avicenna's philosophical encyclopedia was burned on the orders of the caliph of Baghdad in 1150;[147] later, every available copy was destroyed, and only fragments of the original text remain. Averroës's writings were burned while the philosopher was still alive, in 1196, and strict prohibitions were enacted against studying his as well as Greek philosophy. God, as the edict of the caliph of Córdoba puts it, has decreed the fires of hell for those who teach that truth can be found through pure reason.[148] The renegade and mystic al-Ghazali, [513] who appeared on the scene with his *Destructio Philosophorum* against Avicenna and philosophy, with the aim of restoring religion, had an objective ideological stake in such persecution. Philosophy became suspicious in the eyes of the people; in *The Thousand and One Nights*, in which the "sciences" in themselves are still honored, where skills, like the art of poetry, are exalted almost as much as a concubine, Avicenna is remembered only as an evil sorcerer.[149] Philosophy became as dangerous in the Orient as the natural sciences did in Italy after Galileo's trial.[150] To be sure, this has changed to some extent in the modern era; there are glossarists of Avicenna, such as a good Persian one in the seventeenth century;[151] in Cairo, at the greatest Arab university, there have been lectures on Avicenna and Averroës since the nineteenth century,[152] and yet the catechism prevailed on the whole over the Eastern Dr. Faust. It was a double emancipation of Near Eastern peoples—from a half-colonial condition and perhaps from their own intellectual torpor; it is once again possible to hear there the sound of what was tarnished along with Avicenna. It is his fertile, self-theurgic, processual, earthly world,[153] and one that knows, indeed, no colorless, no pulseless matter. Islamic philosophy is certainly not only limited to the Aristotelian Left; Renan even states hyperbolically, "The true philosophical movement of Islamism should be sought in its theological sects."[154] He is here thinking of the Brethren of Purity of Basra yet also of the various teachings like those of the aforementioned *mutakallimūn* and their paradoxical linking of atomism to the sole causality of God.[155] As leaders of sects, moreover, these nonnaturalists were also by no means crown witnesses for orthodoxy, not to mention that there was no philosophically noteworthy theology to speak of at that time in the Orient. Renan therefore stresses something else insofar as he distinguishes between two types of philosophy, the theistic and the naturalistic (with "eternal matter, the seed's evolution through its own latent power"): "Arab philosophy, and in particular that of Ibn Rushd, classes itself in a manner more decidedly in accord with the second of these categories."[156] [514] And, above all, the philosophical-religious sects did not reflect the "true philosophical movement of Islam"; rather, the latter appeared and persisted only in Avicenna and Averroës. The hatred of reason and science recognized this well when it took offense to the work of both and extinguished the light within it. That was its effect on the Islamic orthodoxy, which went so far as to bring the word "falasuf" and philosophy itself into disrepute.

In this case, then, books made humans worse, and yet they sought, with clear instructions, to make them better, with the instruction to sublate this inherited religion not only into knowledge but also, one might now say, into *virtue*.[157] This type of naturalization also belongs, it must be stressed in the end, to the line of thought initially pursued by Avicenna. Just as the theoretical content of religion here goes far beyond its representations and dispenses with them, so the practical content of religion here goes far beyond its rituals and dispenses with them all the more decisively. What remains of morality is, according to Avicenna as well as Averroës, the natural ethical law, with justice as its central virtue. As central, it connects all humans, according to their conscience, independent of their beliefs; it is *the active-universal reason of the species in relation to the will.* Ibn Tufayl, who was determined by Avicenna and linked with Averroës, notably illustrated this natural ethical law above the religions in his *Philosophus Autodidactus*. When his philosophical Robinson returned to be among humans again, he felt an aversion to religious ceremonies—laws, too—and he frowned upon the fact that in these laws, Muhammad allowed humans to have riches and to increase their means. At the same time, however, he conceded that all the wisdom, correction, and improvement of which humans are capable is contained in the words of the prophet and, admittedly, no differently than in Moses and the prophet Jesus. This tolerance is therefore possible because the best thing in religious law is taken to be precisely its nonreligious kernel: ethical life.[158] The main purpose of Ibn Tufayl's novel is just this: to show that a human without awareness of positive religion can not only [515] obtain knowledge of God and nature but also of the wisdom of virtue. The natural ethical law thus applies here as both criterion and sanction and furnishes the content of natural religion in accordance with its practical elements.[159] God's qualities are not his but are instead models for humans, of their disposition and of the activity by which this disposition proves itself. In Maimonides, the Jewish Aristotelian who stands not too far from Avicenna and Averroës, this appeared in his *Guide of the Perplexed* as the idea that our knowledge of God is limited to those attributes that relate exclusively to humans, namely, ethical life.[160] And from here, the influence of Eastern naturalism could also be felt in Europe; on Abelard,[161] on Roger Bacon, and ultimately on the European Enlightenment of the seventeenth and eighteenth centuries. In the place of the Qur'an, Abelard used the Decalogue and the Gospels; both spoke clearly of the goodness inscribed within everyone's conscience. Roger Bacon similarly taught that the ethical law was equally illuminating and substantially identical for all humans; according to him, it would even comprise the substance of any imaginable universal religion in the future.[162] And what does Spinoza, centuries later yet nearer to the oriental cultural circle than any other great thinker, want to show more urgently in his *Theological-Political Treatise* than that the essence of religion does not consist in the acknowledgement of specific dogmas, but rather in humane disposition and the praxis that stems from it?[163] The substance of religious symbols may not be exhausted by morality, but it is insubstantial if it does not contain the humanity that proves itself in morality.[164] All the worse for religion if it contradicts this; all the better for morality if it also brings the humane, deep element in great religious documents out of myth and to the earth.[165] And naturalism stands so little opposed to morality that, precisely because it is the location of this-worldliness, it embraces the fruit in which the goodness of every faith is recognizable. It likewise embraces improvement, which is an earthly path, not a heavenly one. The transformation of religion [516] into improvement intended by Avicenna was founded on natural light; above all, however, it also saw itself on the terrain of a world whose forms are nothing if, within them, no matter forms itself and bears fruit.

ARISTOTLE AND NONMECHANISTIC MATTER

The only fruitful memories are those that remind one of what remains to be done. The Aristotelian Left has been around a long time and was halfway in the grave; today it emerges again for a fresh look, especially its change of the matter-form relationship, in an era in which the question of matter is highly pressing. Hegel is important because of the dialectical method, but Aristotle and his Left are important because of their concept of matter. For them, after all, it is full of movement, full of form, and develops itself *qualitatively* beyond its quantitative foundation. As the substrate of this stepwise development, matter is both *conditioning everything*—"according-to-what-is-considered-possible"—and, above all, *predisposed for everything*—as "what-may-become-possible," as "objective Possibility."[166] This is a richer concept of matter than the purely mechanistic one, although the latter is retained in its proper place, beneath the ongoing qualitative movements, changes, transformations. And [as for] the concept of form in Aristotle, if he had already sought to mediate it with matter through the relational concept of development, the Aristotelian Left subsequently made it an almost entirely immanent mode of existence, a form of existence within matter itself. All this is a hardly sufficiently appreciated chapter in the hardly sufficiently appreciated history of the concept of matter. Forms are material figural constructions,[167] and the movement toward these constructions, through them as always, means not only that movement is an "unfinished entelechy," in Aristotle's profound phrase, but also that each distinct entelechy must be understood as itself still unfinished, as a shape in process, and therefore as a series of experimental shapes, excerpt shapes of matter.[168] And this [is] simply by dint of the continuing "dynamei-on," of "what-may-become-possible," thus of *objective-real possibility, the* [517] *substrate of which constitutes the total matter of existence*, the horizons of which remain incomplete. In mechanistic-static matter, there is no process and no dialectic: the task is therefore also to understand the substrate of the dialectical process in line with the real-possible as always revealing a tendency. The human and physical world effects itself in this manner, in the way that maturation, realization, and dispersal perpetually interact. Its matter is that which further and further shapes itself and can be shaped in accordance with its essential form of existence, and the fulfilled Totum of this form of existence itself may yet become a real possibility, and indeed, only in this manner.[169]

TRANSFORMATION OF ARISTOTLE BY HIS LEFT, TRANSFORMATION OF THIS LEFT ITSELF

The concept of matter and form thus undeniably experienced significant transformations in Aristotle and again (and not much less) in the transformations it experienced in his Left. The first thing to be fully superseded was the *passivum* in the Aristotelian concept of possibility, how it is equated in an entirely abstract way with the concept of matter. The ostensibly merely passive possibility, this purely receptive wax, shows itself as a "predisposition toward something" and not by any means as mere waxness or as absolutely undetermined; rather, it is full of active form, through which the possible actively produces and organizes itself in accord with the new realities pressing forth within it. Yet the concept of material reality must also be significantly changed contra the Aristotelian one: the truly future-bearing grandeur of the thought with which Aristotle depicted possibility in general together with matter consequently appears all the more fertile. The noted displacement of meaning in the Aristotelian synonyms of "predisposition" and "possibility" is itself already predisposed within Aristotle, moreover, and is therefore merely further developed by the Aristotelian Left. This occurs thanks to the sea change introduced by Avicenna, one that reveals the form of matter to be inherently both potential and potent, both potent and potential.

Matter, the Aristotelian Left thus says, is that [518] which bears its idiosyncratic forms within itself and which it brings to realization through its movement. Evidently, this definition—taken over in almost all Renaissance natural philosophy—at once implies a fire, a horizon full of the sheer desire to become.[170] It is true that this blossoming definition did not lend itself to the precision with which the mechanistic concept later distinguished itself, but for that reason, it avoided being only a partial definition of matter, its movements, and its shapes. The Aristotelian Left taught that all forms, even intellectual and organic ones, are included within matter, and this doctrine in nuce already prevented the reduction that the concept of matter underwent with the absolutization of mechanics, or rather, by mechanism.[171] Thus, Marx, in *The Holy Family*, praises the Renaissance dimension of matter, which was already portended in the Aristotelian Left:

> Among the qualities inherent in *matter*, *motion* is the first and foremost, not only in the form of *mechanical* and *mathematical* motion, but chiefly in the form of an *impulse*, a *vital spirit*, a *tension*—or a "*Qual*," to use a term of Jakob Böhme's—of matter. The primary

> forms of matter are the living, individualizing *forces of being* inherent in it and producing the distinctions between the species. In *Bacon*, ... materialism still holds back within itself in a naïve way the germs of a many-sided development. On the one hand, matter, surrounded by a sensuous, poetic glamor, seems to attract man's whole entity by winning smiles. On the other, the aphoristically formulated doctrine pullulates with inconsistencies imported from theology.[172]

Materialism after Hobbes purged the world of whatever it considered inconsistent, yet already in Bruno, the materialist of the natura naturans, this so-called theological inconsistency exists only as pantheism. Otherwise, finally imbued with potency, matter is powerful enough to—as Goethe says—dispense with spirit, which only impels the passive from outside. This is thus the *first transformation of Aristotle* that the Left set in motion: the *activation* of matter.

And yet the fruit of this then-newly obtained matter-form relationship is not yet fully ripened. For—and here is meant the transformation of the Aristotelian Left itself [519]—Bruno's blossoming matter is one that is already completed, taken on the whole. With the doctrine that the universe is completely realized matter-potentiality, Bruno takes both Avicenna and Averroës as thinkers whose form-matter may be developed further toward its own completion. This final *statics* is more conspicuous in Bruno, however, than it is in the actual Aristotelian Left, let alone in Aristotle himself. For if matter, pregnant with forms, perpetually transforming itself, is nonetheless complete on the whole, stands still, then it looks different to the Copernican Bruno, as well as to the cosmologists of an infinite pregnancy of form, than it does to the philosophers of the Middle Ages. Avicenna and Averroës lived in the Ptolemaic system; their matter-form relationship itself was, despite natura naturans, still constructed hierarchically within a world-sphere.[173] Yet even the Copernican Bruno, the thinker of fermenting infinity, allows that the matter of his universe has already completed what it can, with the argument that all possibilities must have already been realized in the whole of the universe, for otherwise, the perfection of this totality would indeed lack a conclusion and would, therefore, not be perfect. Bruno undoubtedly retained for philosophy part of Ptolemy in this Totality-Statics and even added to it for the sake of the theological *Possest*, the absolutely completed "capacity to do," with which Nicholas of Cusa had, a hundred years earlier, defined perfection in his concept of God.[174] With all this, Bruno also inhibited what Marx described as the vigor of Renaissance materialism, which Bruno represented so well: the actual dimension of production. The vigor of Bruno's world, of radical potentiality-potency-matter, certainly beats within the persistent pulse of contradictions and their vitality, but the whole lies still in the pure static harmony of these contradictions, and even makes this statics visible both temporally, in the persistence of objects, and spatially, in the large bodies of the universe. This, however, inhibits precisely the self-shaping possibility or the fullness of life of matter discussed from Avicenna to Bruno; it interrupts that which has not yet been carried to term in its true totality and Totum. Fully realized possibility is not an already-finished [520] Universal-Life that splits the actively conceived dynamei-on in half, if not into another mechanism of unliveliness.[175] This makes the *second transformation* of the grand matter-form tradition inevitable, a transformation that now concerns the *horizon* of matter-possibility and not only its *passivity*. It must be stressed that the posited transformation is already implied in the Aristotelian concept of the *predisposition*, not only as active-dispositional, but also as anticipatory-latent predisposition. And it is precisely its latency, filled with the fermenting future, that constitutes the *fertility* of matter, its capacity to manifest itself in ever-new forms of existence. And not only in ever-new but also in ever-more-specific forms of existence, those that are ever more suited to the not-yet-produced kernel of this existence. In this teleological path of the essential form of existence of that enduring Totum, real possibility is not broken off but realized. That which remains latent in the predisposition of the world in general illuminates, first, the processual labor and wealth of shapes with which the latent progressively produces and manifests itself.[176] But because this is the case, because the corrected concept of possibility in Aristotelian matter offers the best depiction of actual matter-predisposition, the substrate of the forms of existence, in a dialectical process of self-production and the eternal breaking through of itself, may not be circumscribed by the old pan-matter. The highest level of heaven is here not yet exploded, the idolatry of circles is not yet superseded, but Hegel almost brought stability to this process, with a different emphasis, moving from the curvature of space to that of time.[177] The *birth of the new out of the fund of objective-real possibility, out of matter as the substrate of this possibility*, accordingly remained without its own concept. It is only genuine historical-dialectical materialism, properly understood, not the materialism that is still today the usual Eastern fare nor in that which is deployed anew, indeed, forced into barracks, defused, trivialized, and drilled, denied freedom and without openness; only a materialism moved by "the seeds of an all-around development," oriented toward the horizon of the future, provides the remedy. Yet his concept of dialectical [521] matter, with the vigor of its vitality, was and remains indebted to Aristotle, as does the not-yet-completed tradition of the Aristotelian Left. And so here he is remembered—Avicenna's day of commemoration also celebrates an earlier, not-yet-finished view of matter *without mechanism*. It was certainly full of far greater theological inconsistencies than the Renaissance view of matter, yet these were scrutinized and dismissed. What remains most worthy of consideration is dynamei-on as efficacy and seeds—materia universalis, which holds the world together, unfinished, in its innermost and outermost, from beginning to end. Matter, therefore, also has its utopia; in objective-real possibility, it stops being abstract.

ART, RELEASING MATTER-FORM

Human labor steadily develops present existence further.[178] It transforms objects insofar as it redirects them following a set pattern or carries them forward toward our ends. The labor of *artistic* design is distinguished from this only by the nature of the end, one of entertaining and lending significance,[179] toward which it continues to develop what is in its embrace. As the end of entertaining and lending significance always occurs in an essentially clarified or elevated subject, it is necessarily connected to what Avicenna characterized as dispositional matter. Fully in line with the tradition of pregnant form and pointing toward the idea of liberating matter, one of Lessing's observations is apropos. The painter in *Emilia Galotti*, who brings the prince a commissioned painting, speaks Lessing's own thoughts and, indeed, in words that recall Aristotle, or rather Avicenna-Averroës: "Art must paint the picture as Plastic Nature—if there is such a thing—imagined it: without the falling off that recalcitrant matter makes unavoidable, without the decay with which time attacks it."[180] The resistant matter is the material of "what-is-considered-possible," taken as a disruption or constraint; the conjectured plastic nature, however, thinking its own image, this is the material of "what-may-become-possible," [522] which the artist further actualizes. And indeed—pointing directly to the Aristotelian Left—not as passive but as active matter, that is, as natura naturans, which further actualizes its own potency-potentiality in the artist. Present existence is accordingly not slavishly depicted, nor is it violated by imprinted form; instead, that which is predisposed within its matter—perhaps not yet matured to full clarity—is artistically driven to completion. In Lessing's Averroistic dictum, all art is malleably impelled and re-impelled in the formed matter as well as in the formed subject-matter of the object. Indeed, such different thinkers as Schopenhauer and Hegel agree on the idea of the artistic release of forms out of a form-pregnant matter-Nature. Both do so, admittedly, with a relative depreciation of nature, with the transformation of the artist into what remains of the *dator formarum*. Thus, Schopenhauer claims of the artistic genius, it is "as if he *understands nature's half-spoken words*, and then clearly enunciates what nature only stutters, imprinting in solid marble the beauty of the form as if to call out to her: 'This is what you wanted to say!' and

'Yes, that was it!' is the reply of the knowing connoisseur."[181] Hegel, however, despite his resistance to the still-unshaped beauty of nature, confesses in the manner of Lessing: "Now as the pulsating heart shows itself all over the surface of the human, in contrast to the animal, body, so in the same sense it is to be asserted of art that it has to convert every shape in all points of its visible surface into an eye. . . . Thus it can be said of art, it makes every one of its productions into a thousand-eyed Argus, whereby the inner soul and spirit is seen at every point."[182] In this definition, a sort of artistic development of a latent form-content is also clearly described. This, to be sure, is according to the measure of an aesthetic ideal, yet one that is immanently prefigured in active appearances. [523]

The modern artist thus now steps into the scene as both the liberating and perfecting force, such that he clearly and distinctly brings out, exposes, the shape of matter predisposed within matter. Form, "spirituality," becomes thereby identical to the immanent-entelechial type of things, of characters, of situations. Avicenna called form the "fiery truth" of matter; Averroës allowed this truth to increasingly emerge within matter through the "circular motion of the heavens."[183] Of course, the artist finds himself in the Aristotelian Left and, with Giordano Bruno, only as universal or pantheistic natura naturans, not as an individual. The emphasis on the artist himself as the perfecting mover only came into the modern age through the great humanist Julius Caesar Scaliger;[184] and yet Scaliger was devoted to the naturalism of Padua, the high bastion of Averroism. In his influential *Poetics* (1561), Scaliger defined the poet as one who does not imitate nature, "like an actor," but who instead re-creates it and brings it to its end, "like another God," that is, like a Prometheus; so it is that the Typical-Real emerges "without impediments" out of the presently existing.[185] The Typical-Real is the "species,"[186] or the predisposed entelechial form; put in good Averroist fashion: "In ipsis naturae normis atque dimensionibus universa perfectio est."[187] In the context of Scaliger's Prometheus-artist, this means that artistic beauty involves creatively giving shape to the indicated perfection of the norms and dimensions of matter-nature.

Here, along with the implication of the line from Lessing, lies the *aesthetic* afterripening of the Aristotelian Left, that is, its doctrine that art is capable of releasing the form within pregnant matter. With regard to the sought Typical,[188] this results from the Aristotelian claim that poetry is more philosophical than the writing of history, for it features more general validity (the total unity of that which is the ongoing issue),[189] whereas the writing of history features more of the particular.[190] This, finally, holds together with the Aristotelianism of Goethe (in *Diderot's Essay on Painting*), when he [524] follows nature and calls on painters not to depict but to further develop what is immanent: "And so the artist, thankful of the nature that also produced him, gives back to her a second nature, but one felt, one thought, one humanly completed."[191] And this reminder also illuminates that the task of open entelechy, placed properly on its feet, is not at an end, at least with regard to aesthetic realism, so very different from the witlessness of imitation or all the lies of embellishment. The art that creates is preshaped as a realistic ideal; it makes the Typical-Meaningful discernible, just as it also encourages and emboldens what has not yet become possible in active reality. The matter-form concept, naturalistically interpreted, as in Avicenna, demands a broader Left philosophy as the philosophy of dialectical-material *tendency and latency alike*. In the same vein, the womb of matter is not yet exhausted by what has hitherto come into being; the most important forms of existence of its history and nature still remain in the latency of real possibility. This most important thing,[192] historically self-mediating, appears as a realistic ideal and precisely as the possibility of an open reality, one that is immanent in unfinished matter. The dynamei-on has more than enough room for the realistic ideal; its form is only that which Avicenna called "the fiery truth of matter." This, with an echo of Heraclites's fire—not as the "essence" of things, but rather in that they are on fire like a stove, and thus the essence of its matter decocts itself, ripens. [525]

TEXTUAL PASSAGES AND ANNOTATIONS

ARISTOTLE

"Light too makes colors which are potential into actual colors."
 On the Soul 3.5 (430a16)[193]*

"Now we speak of one particular kind of existent things as substance, and under this heading we so speak of one thing *qua* matter, which in itself is not a particular, another *qua* shape and form, in virtue of which it is then spoken of as particular, and a third *qua* the product of these two. And matter is potentiality, while form is actuality."
 On the Soul 2.1 (412a5)[194]

"There are as many kinds of movement and change as of being. Each kind of thing being divided into the potential and the fulfilled, I call the actuality of the potential as such, movement. . . . Movement takes place when the fulfillment itself exists, and neither earlier nor later. The fulfillment then, of that which is potentially, when it is fulfilled and actual, not *qua* itself, but *qua* moveable, is movement."
 Metaphysics K.9 (1065b14–24)[195]

---

* In the passages that follow, ellipses in square brackets ([. . .]) indicate Bloch's omissions, braces ({ }) indicate Bloch's insertions, and double square brackets ([[ ]]) indicate editorial emendations in the English translations employed here.

AVICENNA

"The philosophical sciences [...] are divided into the {theoretical}[196] and the practical. [...] The *theoretical* {which is divided into mathematics, natural sciences, and metaphysics} are those wherein we seek the perfecting of the theoretical faculty of the soul through the attainment of the intellect in act—this by the attainment of conceptual and verifiable knowledge through things that are [[the things]] they are, without [[reference to their]] being our [[own]] actions and states. [...] [P]*ractical* philosophy {Ethics} is that wherein one first seeks the perfection of the theoretical faculty by [526] attaining conceptual and verifiable knowledge involving things that are [[the things]] they are in being our own actions—thereby attaining, secondly, the perfection of the practical faculty through morals.... Metaphysics {the final part of theoretical philosophy}[197] is the science in which the first causes of natural and mathematical existence and what relates to them are investigated (as a *problem*).[198] [...]

"What adheres necessarily to this science is that it is necessarily divided into parts. Some of these will investigate the ultimate causes [...] from which emanates every caused existent.[199] [...] Some will investigate the accidental occurrences to the existent {Prior, Posterior, Potency and Act, the Whole and the Part, Individuality, Difference, Antitheses, and more}, and some the principles of the particular sciences. And because the principles of each science that is more particular are things searched after in the higher science—as, for example, the principles of medicine in natural [[science]] and of surveying in geometry—it will so occur in this science that the principles of the particular sciences that investigate the states of the particular existents are clarified therein. [...] From the above, the purpose of this science has become manifest and apparent."

The Metaphysics of the Healing, 2, 11–12 (1.1, 1.2)[200]

"With every originated thing, before its origination, it is in itself such that it is possible for it to exist or impossible for it to exist."
The Metaphysics of the Healing, 140 (4.2)[201]

The same claim, further explained, against the assumption that pure potentiality does not exist because it does not become actual:
"As for the nature of that which is potential, its receptacle is {exclusively}[202] matter. Thus, it is matter that is properly said to exist in itself in potentiality and in actuality through form."
The Metaphysics of the Healing, 70 (2.4)[203]
[527]

Material potentiality does, indeed, not actualize by itself—it is not the cause of the *existence* of forms. The material cause is merely one condition for the possibility of a thing's *predisposed content* coming into being:
"As for matter, it cannot be the cause for the existence of form. For, first of all, matter is only matter because it has the potency to receive and to be disposed to receive. But that which is disposed to receive, inasmuch as it is disposed, is not the cause for the existence of that for which it is disposed. If it were such a cause, then that which it received must exist permanently for it, without there being any disposition for its reception. Second, it is impossible for a thing's essence, when still in potentiality, to be the cause of something in actuality."
The Metaphysics of the Healing, 65 (2.4)[204]

A more precise description of the material cause, one that portrays matter-potency as predisposed. These dispositions (predispositions)[205] unmistakably vary in form according to their content (here Avicenna speaks for himself, and not by any means Aristotelicissime):[206]
"As regards the material cause (*causa materialis*),[207] it is that wherein is the potentiality of a thing's existence. We say: a thing may have this state in conjunction with another thing in several ways:

"Sometimes it is as the tablet is to writing—namely, in that it is disposed to receive something that may occur to it without this involving change in it or the disappearance of a state belonging to it because of the writing. Sometimes it is as the piece of wax is to its carved image, and the boy to the man—namely, in that it is disposed to receive something that occurs to it, without there being a change in its state except for motion, in place, in quantity, or some other similar thing. [528] Sometimes it is as the piece of wood is to the bed, for the carpenter diminishes some of the wood's substance through chiseling. Sometimes it is as the black thing to the white, for it changes and loses its quality without losing its substance. [. . .] Sometimes it is like sperm is to the animal, for it needs to divest itself from a number of forms belonging to it so as to become disposed to receive the animal form. The same applies to unripe grapes in relation to wine. Sometimes the *causa materialis* is as prime matter is to form, for it is disposed to receive it, to become rendered subsistent by it in act. Sometimes it is as myrobalan to the confection,[208] for it is not from it alone that the confection comes to be, but from it and from another. Prior to this, it would have been one of its parts in potency. Sometimes it is as wood and stone are to the house. This is similar to the former example, except that in the case of the former, the confection comes about through some mode of transformation, whereas in this case there is only composition. [. . .]

"It is, hence, in these ways that we find the things that carry potentiality. For they either bear potentiality singly or with the participation of others. If they bear it singly, then this takes place in one of two alternatives. One is where that which comes about from them will need only to become actual for being this thing alone. This is the thing which, properly speaking, ought to be called subject with respect to that which is in it. A thing of this sort must have self-subsistence in actuality. For, if it did not have subsistence, it would be impossible for it to be prepared for the reception of what occurs in it. On the contrary, it must be subsistent in actuality. For if it becomes subsistent only through that which comes to inhere in it, [529] then something through which it has become subsistent must already have come to inhere in it before the second came to inhere in it. Either the second thing would then be among the things that do not render it subsistent but are something added to it, or else its arrival would annul that which previously rendered it subsistent. But then the thing would have been transformed when we have supposed it not to have been transformed. This, then, is one alternative. The second alternative is that the bearer needs an additional thing. The need would either be only for a motion, whether locomotion, qualitative motion, quantitative motion (positional or substantial), or due to the loss of something else from its substance by way of quantity, quality, or the like.

"As for the material cause,[209] by participating with another, it necessarily has combination and composition. The composition will consist either of combination alone or, in addition to this, there would be qualitative transformation. Everything that has change in it attains the end either through one alternation or through numerous alterations."[210]

The Metaphysics of the Healing, 215–17 (6.4)[211]

Reasserting matter's development toward its essential form, matter is not only determinant quantitatively but also qualitatively:

"In brief, even though the material form is a cause of matter in that it actualizes and perfects it, matter also has an influence in its existence—namely, in rendering it specific and making it concrete. [. . .] [E]ach of the two is necessarily a cause of the other in one thing, but not in one [530] respect. If it were not for this, it would be impossible for the material form to have, in any manner whatsoever, a connection with matter. For this reason we have previously said that form alone is not sufficient for the existence of matter, but rather, form is part of the cause. If this, then, is the case, then it is impossible to make form a cause of matter in all respects, form being in no need of anything other than itself."

The Metaphysics of the Healing, 329 (9.4)[212]

The body is the unity of matter and form as a physical object. Yet Avicenna wants to understand *this body as not determined only in three dimensions*. At the very least, the body's dimensions are modifiable, and thus, these dimensions are not essential to it. It is likewise inessential that a body be "above" or "below," aside from the fact that it exists below the heavens and thus must be finite. What is essential for a body—beyond these relative aspects—is simply that it exists in the form of continuity, which is capable of discarding particular dimensions. Thus, embodiment is presented implicitly as *not necessarily involving a res extensa or only admitting of quantitative accounts.* This is rather deeper than the prevailing conception of extension, and also exists in nonquantitative appearances:

"It is not a {necessary} condition for the body to be a body that it should have unequal dimensions...."[213] Nor, moreover, is its being a body dependent on its being placed under the heaven so that the different directions would obtain for it in accordance with the direction of the world.... This, then, is how body should be defined—namely, that it is the substance that has the form by virtue of which it is what it is and that the rest of the dimensions postulated between its limits, and also its limits, its shapes, and its position, are not matters that render it subsistent but are, rather, sequels to its substance.... For corporeality, in reality, is the form of a continuum that is receptive of the hypothesized three dimensions of which we spoke."

There is an early Leibniz in these dynamic determinations first posited of space, a significant [531] expansion of the concept of *esse corpus* behind and beyond the quantitative.[214]

The Metaphysics of the Healing, 49–51 (2.2)[215]

AVERROËS

The understanding can only perceive universal forms, yet these only appear within material plurality. If the understanding can nonetheless grasp this material plurality, assuming it is not unpredicable,[216] then the intelligible forms must not lie outside of material plurality.[217] This plurality would otherwise be unintelligible,[218] for there would only be knowledge of universal forms, not of worldly things. That such knowledge does exist, however, shows that forms themselves live in matter; thus, the understanding can grasp them as many:

"As for the thesis of a numerical plurality of immaterial souls, this is not a theory acknowledged by the philosophers, for they regard matter as the cause of numerical plurality and form as the cause of congruity in numerical plurality. And that there should be a numerical plurality without matter, having one unique form, is impossible."

The Incoherence of the Incoherence, 14 (1.26–27)[219]

Matter as potentiality is neither unpredicable nor ghostly; rather, it really exists. And its real substrate: material cannot itself not-have-been in a given prior moment;[220] that is, it cannot have just been created. Possibility, receptive capacity, potentiality, and materiality are all uncreated, for if they were created, then the act of their creation would have made something from that which was not potential, which is impossible. Consequently, matter does not need a creator in order to exist; instead, it is, together with the movement within it, eternal. In this way, material is neither capable of nor requires creation; a preworldly, eternal Allah apart from worldly-eternal matter cannot be proven:

"Possibility needs something for its subsistence.[221] ... Thus the possibility of the patient [532] is a necessary condition for the possibility of the agent,[222] for the agent which cannot act is not possible but impossible. ... There must, therefore, be an eternal movement which produces this interchange in the eternally transitory things;[223] [. . .] for the meaning of 'becoming' is the alteration of a thing, and its change, from what it has potentially, into actuality. ... There exists, therefore, a substratum for the contrary forms, and it is in this substratum that the forms interchange."

The Incoherence of the Incoherence, 59–60 (1.101–2)[224]

The guiding of the possible to the actual already begins within the potential, which is, as such, the womb of the actual. In matter, the forms themselves mature as dispositional and latent, and the act (at its highest conceived of as an unmoved mover) can bring nothing new into the world; it only realizes what is already latent. Averroës makes this clear in his long commentary on Aristotle's *Metaphysics* (in his explanation of book Λ, chapter 3):[225] the cause of motion does not give things their forms, but is rather *the mere eductor of form*, bringing to light the forms that already lie in the matter (*non dat, sed extrahit*).[226] Thus souls and ideas are similarly already latent as forms in matter, and indeed in such a manner that they—like everything materially latent—do not involve a merely passive potentiality but a suo genere active potentiality.[227] This capacity to mature forms to their actualization, that is, to develop them to the point where they spring from potentiality into something real, considerably expands the notion of potential: as an active disposition, potentiality becomes incubation, becomes the womb of a natura naturans. At the same time, this expansion introduces not only forms, but also the actualizing principles within them,[228] into Aristotelian *dynamis*. In Greek, dynamis has a double meaning: to be possibility and potency, potentiality and capacity.[229] The sharp logicians Avicenna and Averroës noted this double meaning (echoed in the Arabic)—they did not fall victim to the assumption that the term is simply linguistically ambiguous. [533] (In *The Incoherence of the Incoherence*, Averroës explicitly distinguishes the two meanings of dynamis: "For it must not be believed that the possibility of the recipient is the same as the possibility of the agent. It is a different thing to say about Zaid, the agent, that he can do something, and to say about the patient that it can have something done to it.")[230] Hence, Averroës, far from inscrutable equivocation, thoroughly embraced the passive-active double meaning of dynamis-matter. Precisely the specific "potency" of form development now pulsates within the general "potentiality" of matter and makes dynamis-matter the womb of the undeveloped yet maturing configurations of form.

As a consequence, there occurs a revision of Aristotle's other concept of matter, of that what-is-considered-possible (kata to dynaton) alongside what-may-become-possible (dynamei-on). That is to say, it is precisely conditioning potency that determines the sequence of prior and posterior in appearances. In this vein, Averroës distinguished a "proximate or remote potency" in material dispositions, corresponding to the prior or posterior of possible actualization. As such, in no way are all things possible at any given time; rather, there is—as a result of "proximate or remote potency"—a developmental road map, the stations of which cannot be skipped. In this way, the *temporal sequence* of the form-content—not just the content itself—is also predisposed within the potentiality-potency of matter. Of course, this idea does not appear in Aristotle with such clarity; it ultimately contains nothing less than the recognition of a specific mediation of progress, one that is necessary at every point and is determined by the maturity of the conditions. In his short commentary on Aristotle's *Metaphysics*, Averroës explains, with special emphasis on the historical prior and posterior of the actualization of forms:

"As it has become plain what potentiality and actuality are, we shall now state when each particular thing is in potentiality and when it is not; for not anything whatsoever is anything in potentiality. Evidently, there are proximate potentialities as well as remote ones; and, if this is the case, there are [[correspondingly]] remote and proximate substrates. Remote potentialities are not turned into actuality until, through the establishment of the ultimate substrate, the proximate potentiality has been established. Hence, if one states that one thing exists in another in potentiality, while this potentiality is a remote [[potentiality]], this is stated metaphorically. . . . It does not inhere in this substrate in any chance disposition, but only when this is in a disposition in which it is possibly turned into actuality. E.g., semen is said to be man in potentiality when it is introduced into the uterus without coming into contact with air from outside, so that it might be cooled and changed. . . . Hence, the proximate potentiality necessarily requires two things in order to exist at a given time, namely the existence of the proximate substrate, and the disposition in which it is [[actually]] potential. When these two things are given and the efficient causes are complete and nothing [[external]] hinders them, then the thing is turned into actuality by necessity."²³¹

Averroës on Aristotle's Metaphysics, 100–101 (j103)²³²

Averroës made further use of the double meaning already present in Aristotle, that the concept of matter can also mean something formed if that formed thing makes possible a higher formed thing.²³³ Consequently, something can be a form in one relation (like lumber in relation to the act of building), while being matter in another relation (the same lumber in relation to a house). Averroës almost insists upon letting matter and form swap faces, as it were; in any case, matter, which in the form of lumber incorporates a new form, reaches up to the top floor of the world building:

"'Matter' is predicated with respect to [[different]] levels. One of these is first matter, i.e., [[matter]] without form; another is [[matter]] with form, as in the case of the four elements, which [535] [[serve as]] matter for combined bodies. This kind of matter is of two types, firstly the one just mentioned, which is distinguished by [[the fact]] that the form in these [[elements]] is not entirely destroyed when receiving another form, but rather the form of the matter is found in them in some intermediate state. [. . .] In the second type, the form of the matter remains [[the same]] when a second form occurs in it, such as the disposition to receive a soul, which is found in certain homoeomeric bodies. It is especially this [[type of matter]] to which [[one refers by]] the term 'substrate.'"

Averroës on Aristotle's Metaphysics, 48–49 (j55–56)²³⁴

AVICEBRON

The concept of matter was also elevated in a manner different from that of the pregnant Possible.²³⁵ Avicebron taught of a "universal matter," which includes the corporeal as well as the spiritual. Avicebron, the thinker of this "universal matter," did not primarily emanate from Aristotle. He stands significantly more within those Neoplatonist traditions that do not just cover Aristotle up, as sometimes happens in Avicenna and Averroës, but instead engage him directly. Thus Avicebron's highest matter composes itself within universal matter: the "*material spiritualis*," taken directly from Plotinus, namely his "*hyle noetike*," spiritual or intelligible matter (*The Enneads* 2.4.1–5), high above, with the One.[236] In Plotinus's system of emanations, from the One down into the darkness of common matter, the very principle of matter he otherwise vilifies is surprisingly ennobled. This happened because matter became linked with the second-highest thing in Plotinus's world, *nous*, or World Spirit,[237] and so, in the heavenly sphere, lay at the feet of the Highest, the One. And indeed, this was accompanied by the emphatically positive reversal of its absolutely miserable connotation in the lowest world: to be an empty, dark abyss. Precisely this emptiness, impersonal and without quality,[238] could serve as a foil to the most sublime emptiness, qualityless, impersonal, of the One.

"The Mind, too, as also a Reason-Principle, sees only in each particular object the Reason-Principle lodging there; anything lying below that it declares to lie below the light, to be therefore a thing of darkness.... The dark element in the Intelligible, [536] however, differs from that in the sense-world: so, therefore, does the Matter—as much as the forming-Idea presiding in each of the two realms ... There [above], on the contrary, the shape is a real-existent as is the Base. Those that ascribe Real Being to Matter must be admitted to be right as long as they keep to the Matter of the Intelligible Realm: for the Base there is Being, or even, taken as an entirety with the higher that accompanies it, is illuminated Being."

The Enneads, 107[239]

Plotinus's *nous*, or heavenly spirit, is replete with this matter, however, for this *nous* itself constitutes the passive dynamis as the basis for the active dynamis of the One, the Usia.[240] It undoubtedly still seems strange how in Plotinus, the strongest spiritualistic metaphysics, with sensible matter within the damned abyss, allows a similar matter named "substance" to appear again in the intellectual ether. And Avicebron's concept of the "*material spiritualis*" comes directly from this *"hyle noetike"* or *"hyle theia,"* from Plotinus's spiritual, even divinely named matter.

Avicebron's *comprehensive* concept of the "materia universalis" does not derive from Neoplatonism, however. Neither does the matter-form concept of Aristotelian stamp that appears many times in his work *Fons Vitae*. (Which is why the Christian Scholastics—above all, Albertus Magnus—mainly referred to this work by the title *De materia et forma*). Thus, Avicebron still belongs in the Aristotelian Left, not least because of his influence. And in regard to the materia universalis, how it encompasses both corporeal and intelligible matter, how it ultimately comprises the substrate of the unitary structure of the world,[241] Avicebron shows himself to have a far more concrete connection to the peripatetic Strato, and especially to the philosophers of the Stoa, who had indeed long been influenced by Strato,[242] than to Neoplatonism. This despite the system of emanations that one finds especially pronounced in Avicebron, and even despite the extraordinary, wholly matter-free transcendence of "God's Will" that likewise dominates Avicebron's teachings. Beneath this Will, however, in the [537] present world, Avicebron's matter is nearly identical with the essence of things. Here, it is that being that becomes real immediately with the positing of the divine Will; in this manner, matter is both the starting point of and the reason for all finite substances. Those are the main theses of *Fons Vitae*; they could not help but lay the basis for a *Deus sive natura*:[243]

"If everything that exists is continuous and extended from the higher extreme all the way to the lowest extreme and the lowest extreme is composed of matter and form, it is consequently established that everything from the beginning of the higher extreme all the way to the lowest extreme is also composed of matter and form."

The Font of Life, 196[244]

"And according to the ordering of the parts of matters and forms in the intelligible world with the matters and forms in the sensible world and their ordering to one another until there is made

from them a universal sensible matter, a universal sensible form, there will similarly also be an ordering of universal intelligible matter with universal sensible matter and of universal intelligible form with universal sensible form—et fient ambae materiae una materia, et fient utraeque formae una forma. [Both matters will become one matter, and both forms will become one form.]"
 The Font of Life, 197[245]

"Universal matter and universal form are the constituents of the world spirit—scilicet qua substantia intelligentiae est composita ex eis [indeed, because the substance of intelligence has been composed from these things]."
 The Font of Life, 215, 25[246]

"The matter and the form of the world spirit are the starting point of all other matter and form, all the way to the end—et secundum hoc imaginaberis extensionem materiae et formae a supremo usque infinum extensionem unam continuam [According to this, you will imagine the extension of matter and form from the highest all the way to the lowest as one continuous expression]."
 The Font of Life, 246[247]

"Si una est materia universalis omnium rerum, hae proprietates adhaerent ei: scilicet quod sit per se existens, unius essentiae, sustinens diversitatem, dans omnibus essentiam suam et nomen—If there is one universal matter of all things, [538] these properties adhere to it: namely, that it exists through itself, has one essence, sustains diversity, and gives its own essence and name to all things."
 The Font of Life, 69[248]

GIORDANO BRUNO

"Customary belief, Aristotle says in the conclusion to the second Book of Wisdom,[249] is the main obstacle hindering the human understanding from perceiving in experience so many things that are evident in themselves. The magnitude of the power of such custom, he says, is demonstrated by the laws, the validity of which rests far more on fantastic and childish customs than on clear facts. As Aristotle's commentator Averroës remarked on this point, just as humans can so accustom themselves to poison that it becomes as refreshing as a natural drink, it is, on the other hand, possible that what is healthy and enlivening to everyone else becomes harmful to them.

"Those, however, whom fate equipped with greater intellectual gifts, who are no dummies, can catch the light that pours everywhere without much difficulty if they only call for a reckoning concerning the conflict between faith and reason, and anointed as judge between the two adversaries, stepping forward out of the fog of common prejudice, attentively listen to each party's arguments and carefully examine and compare and weigh with a precise scale everything that appears to the senses, be it evident, irrefutable, granted, or established, amenable and customary, as soon as it is nevertheless thrown into doubt, with that which might seem absurd to the opponent. For only in this way will they finally no longer be blind in the eyes of the gods and humans, like the lowly rabble, like the slavish and dumb herd in the deepest darkness and in the dim dungeon of unknowing, but instead can affirm their views in the bright daylight of truth,[250] just like all those who are convinced of the existence of a divine truth. [. . .] [539]

"We stand here, however, in a place where freedom of thought prevails, where each individual should be mindful that his gift of corporeal and spiritual sight are not bestowed for naught, that he does not need to shut his eyes according to the wishes of court jesters and ignoramuses, that he does not ungratefully, and against the generous creator of nature, scorn the gift of reason, as when one does not allow for it to unite with other gifts of the same divinity, and as if one truth could stand in the way of another, as if one true light could eclipse another true light. Should we here be horrified and hide from this capacity to discriminate and examine, the most valuable kernel of our essence, what we might even call 'our very selves'? Rather, being conscious of the divinity that inhabits us and the light that radiates in the fortress of our spirit lets us turn our inquiring eyes in its direction, where, once we look closer, we will assuredly acquire knowledge of its beauty, holiness, and truth, in the face of whose naturalness any deceitful sophism disappears and the superstition of dreaming soothsayers collapses.

"From now on, spirit, aware of its own power, will dare take flight into the infinite, where before it was locked in the smallest dungeon, from which it was only through cracks and crannies, as it were, that it could direct the vision of its short-sighted eyes to the most distant glimmers of the stars—on top of this, its wings were somewhat clipped by the knife of dull customary belief, which put a smokescreen between us and the grandeur of envious gods, a bank of clouds created by its own imagination,[251] and which it took to be made of earth and steel. Liberated, however, from this horror of mortality, of destiny's wrath, of heavy judgment, from the chains of the terrible Erinyes and the conceits of partiality, it leaps into the ether, floats through the unbounded space of such large and countless worlds, visits the stars, and flies beyond the imagined limits of the Everything. The walls of its eighth, ninth, tenth, and other spheres, the blind madness on which the philosophers and mathematicians pride themselves, have disappeared. With the help of [540] inquiry led simultaneously by the senses and by reason, the locks of truth will be opened, the blind will see, the mute will regain their tongues, those who have been hitherto crippled in their spiritual progress will find new strength to seek out the sun, the moon, and other residences in the house of the All-Father, similar to this world that we inhabit, smaller and worse, but also larger and better, in infinite gradation. Thus, we arrive at a more dignified view of divinity and this mother Nature, in whose womb we are produced, preserved, and taken back again, and in the future we will no longer believe that any body can exist without a soul, or indeed, as many falsely claim, that *matter is nothing more than a cesspool of chemical stuff.*"[252]

The Awakener, 120–21, 126–27[253]

That which the forms do not give but instead bring to light out of the inherent within matter is, in Bruno, now entirely natura naturans. It is related to matter (in an image that already appears in Averroës) like a helmsman to a ship, albeit one living completely within it. Thanks in part to productive misunderstandings, Bruno has many ancient philosophers besides Aristotle, including the pre-Socratic hylozoists (vital materialists),[254] attest to the "intimate union of matter and universal form." They thus attest to the matter-form relationship that derives from, as Bruno recognizes, "Aristotle and his kind":[255]

"As for the efficient cause, I saw that the universal physical efficient cause is the universal intellect, which is the first and principal faculty of the world soul, which, in turn, is the universal form of it. [. . .]

"The universal intellect is the innermost, most real, and most proper faculty or potential part of the world soul. It is that one and the same thing that fills everything, illuminates the universe, and directs nature to produce her various species suitably. It is to the production of natural things what our [541] intellect is to the production of the representations of things. The Pythagoreans call it the 'mover' and 'agitator of the universe.' As the poet has expressed:

"'. . . pervading its members, mind stirs the whole mass and mingles with the whole body' (Virgil, *Aeneid* 6.726–27).

"The Platonists call it 'world artificer.' They believe that it proceeds from the higher world, which is indeed one, to this sensible world, which is divided into many, and where, because of the separations of its parts, both harmony and discord reign. This intellect, infusing and instilling something of its own into matter, while itself remaining immobile and undisturbed, produces all things. The hermeticists say that it is 'most fecund in seeds' or yet that it is the 'seed sower' because it impregnates matter with all forms, which, according to their nature and manner of being, succeed in shaping, forming, and weaving matter in ways that are so remarkable and numerous that they cannot be ascribed to chance nor to any other principle incapable of differentiation and arrangement.[256] Orpheus calls it 'the eye of the world,' because it sees both the inside and outside of all natural things in order that they may succeed in producing and maintaining themselves in their proper proportions, intrinsically as well as extrinsically. Empedocles calls it 'the differentiator' since it never tires of distinguishing the forms confused within nature's bosom and of summoning the generation of one from the corruption of another. Plotinus says it is 'the father and progenitor,' because it distributes seeds in nature's field and is the proximate dispenser of forms. As for us, we call it the 'internal artificer,' because it shapes matter, forming it from inside like a seed or root shooting forth and unfolding the trunk, from within the trunk thrusting out the boughs, from inside the boughs the derived branches, and unfurling buds from within these. From therein it forms, fashions, and weaves, as with nerves the leaves, flowers, and fruits, [542] and it is from the inside that, at certain times, it calls back its sap from the leaves and the fruits to the twigs, from the twigs to the branches, from the branch to the trunk, from the trunk to the root."[257]

It is not by chance that material development is expressed here by the ancient image of a tree. Bruno gives new sap to the Scholastic, often-so-dry-seeming concepts when he takes them on. And it is undeniable that this sap, insofar as it tastes pagan, also contains some mythical elements, albeit with the poison removed. Thus, the image of the world tree so appears in almost all astral myths and is rooted in the abyss of earthly powers. Indeed, it also points to the Greek [concept of] matter-terminus—*hyle*—externalized to wood, lumber to rooted forest, the Latin—*material* (probably first used philosophically by Lucretius)—composes itself fully in terms of "Mater," and neither in Aristotle nor in Bruno is this rooted, tree-like, womb character forgotten. Echoes of such a so-to-speak "chthonically" conceived materialism can even be found in Lucretius, when he nonetheless opens his amythical, disenchanting didactic poem *On the Nature of Things* with an appeal to Venus as the all-Mother of Being, as a mythically described natura naturans in the tree of life.²⁵⁸ Tellingly, in the fourth dialogue of Bruno's *Della causa principio ed uno*, it is the obnoxious, unphilosophical pedant Poliinnio, in particular, who lays into woman, mother, and matter with equal saplessness: "It is not without good reason that the senators of Pallas's realm have judged it well to set matter and woman side by side."²⁵⁹ At the same time, the force of this ancient equivalence, bound up with the even older tree archetype, is so strong that the image of a blossoming, fruit-bearing tree-matter positively imposed itself everywhere that matter—under oriental influence—was represented as One in all created things, be they of corporeal or spiritual nature. Hence, despite everything else in the great late Scholastic Duns Scotus, he also anticipates, with explicit reference [543] to Avicebron's *"materia universalis,"* Bruno's tree image, as he confirms it in its consequences. For Duns Scotus writes likewise in "De rerum principio" (quaestio 8, art. 4):²⁶⁰

"Ex his apparet, quod mundus est arbor quaedam pulcherrima, cujus radix et seminarium est materia prima, folia fluentia sunt accidentia, frontes et rami sunt creata corruptibilia, flos anima rationalis, fructus natura angelica."

"The world is a magnificent tree, whose roots and seeds are prime matter, whose leaves are the transient accidents, whose branches and twigs are the ephemeral creations, whose flowers are the rational souls, and whose fruits, finally, are the pure spirits."²⁶¹

In the same passage, Duns Scotus says: "Ego autem ad positionem Avicembronis redeo"²⁶²—hence the tree concept *"materia universalis,"* common to both Scotus and Bruno, is here also consciously attributed to Avicebron. Duns Scotus is otherwise located squarely in the light of church doctrine, with the theism of the day, while the Beyond and dualism completely cease in Bruno's eternal material-world tree. And it is indeed remarkable, if inherently necessary by force of the archetype's nature itself, that the tree metaphor, which reaches backward from Bruno to Duns Scotus and beyond, turns up as well almost word-for-word in Jacob Böhme,²⁶³ who, however, barely knew these literary sources. In the "Preface" to his *Aurora*, Böhme nonetheless characterizes the world almost exactly like Duns

Scotus, and certainly like Bruno, as a tree, permeated from its roots to its flowers and fruits by one sap of life, shaped from the inside outward by its own germinating capacity and subdivided. The issuing powers of the "*corpus naturae*" ascend here as in a tree, or as Schelling would later take up this image, in an "organism" Nature, which opened its own eyes in humans. In all of this, anyway, *immanence* was victorious, and indeed as special, up on high, qualified, and thus did not, in all the tropical wildness, lose connection with the colorful sobriety of the old Left Aristotelians in all their consequences. Now form does not remain external to matter, as the scholastics of the Right had taught, but rather, to summarize once again: matter and form, the capacity to become and [544] the capacity to act, appear bound up in the same natura naturans. If anything, they implicate themselves in a reciprocity in which the passive and the active potency ultimately collapse into one, according to their nature.[264] And so the struggle between idealism and materialism, which the Aristotelian Left fought in its own way (and which, indeed, does not consist of murder, but rather the inheritance of idealism, wherever it was productive, progressive)—this fight is in Bruno clearly for the sake of explaining existence that has emerged from itself. Avicenna becomes more decisive in Averroës, Averroës more decisive in Bruno; philosophy now also increasingly conquers that most sublime spiritual knowledge known as that of pure form.

To no longer discard matter, but to always develop it deeper, is imperative from now on. The main point about Bruno is that that he maintains the unity of form (the active principle) and matter, that matter is productive in itself. This is a grand definition,[265] with notable influence, initiated by Avicenna, left incomplete by Bruno. And yet the human in the natura naturans is missing in it; the entire aspect of the labor and history that effects the progress of nature is missing; above all, character—limited by class status as well as the completed Pan of Pantheism—is missing: an unfinished world. But just as in Bruno's torrent of life, the storm of actions is thoroughly dialectical, the acutely pursued tension and unity of opposites, so, too, does this dynamic weaving have a supple matter as its substrate, one considered capable of development and qualification. All this results in important points that are difficult to assess; although they still lie partly on this side of advanced consciousness,[266] they strike a heavy blow against a narrow mechanism. Therefore we can now say: *Hegel is important because of the dialectical method (and everything connected with it), but Aristotle and his Left are important because of their concept of matter.* Not only Hegel; the Aristotelian matter-concept and its radicalizing (penetrating to the roots) Avicenna-Bruno metamorphosis are alive in dialectically conceived materialism, an especially noteworthy ferment. They promote the development of the *world*-image, better yet, the true [545] *meta*-physics of activity and hope, in contradistinction to the purely or impurely mechanical, that of stasis and the absence of qualities. Spirit, moreover, as the highest bloom of organic matter, would not be able to arise from it [matter] and transform existence if it were not required and called forth by it, thus, if it were not predisposed within it, and lastly, autochthonous. It is likewise enclosed by its own matter, for the latter itself possesses emergent consciousness as its own and forms the logical-dialectical process figures as its own in-formation. This expansion and creative reclamation of a concept of matter does not sublate the diversity of its fields and layers; quite the contrary. It offers a common starting point for the particular chemical, organic, psychic, socioeconomic, and cultural modes, forms of organizing the world's matter. The denial of this [reality], against all appearances, was reserved only for the mechanists, ultimately the vulgar materialists. It is entirely different, however, with the bad—or rather, bad-dualist—distinction that came to be employed between matter and spirit, between *hyle* and *pneuma*. A barren matter, to which everything "leads back," a truncated spirit, to which everything is overstretched and "elevated," is the result. Rather, the problem facing the left Aristotelians, still unsatisfied, remains more pressing than ever: how, in material events and their forms, transformations do not to lose the Topos, in which colors as well as the qualities of things do not become corrupted, in which life, consciousness, the path of human history, and its creations have a place against and within this enormous inorganic background. In one gesture, we can say that material utopia is not really a paradox, that dynamei-on matter implies a total concrete-utopian content, and we can hold its latent form as a foundation. Avicenna and Averroës themselves, having unbound themselves and embraced transformation, had bestowed on their *eductio formarum ex materia* not only a hylozoist but also *hylokryphe*, thus latent form, an "incomplete entelechy." For all formations are attempts to shape the not-yet-actualized treasury of matter itself—without an inert mechanical block standing against it and without a prime mover floating above it. This is, or rather this is helped by, the speculative materialism of the Aristotelian Left, which is certainly not yet at its end, despite all its talk of the completed seventh day and its pantheistic claims that we have reached our final day of rest in the dynamei-on itself, as though Pan were both good and all that were needed. Yet there is no way out of this closed system, in particular in its surplus dimensions: eschatological profundity cannot be fulfilled without Bruno and Spinoza, and without this other thing, namely, a conscience that is turned outward against both subjectivism and mechanistic dogma.

NOTES

A NOTE ON THE TEXT AND TRANSLATION

1. Ernst Bloch, "Avicenna und die Aristotelische Linke," *Sinn und Form* 4, no. 3 (1952): 8–59.
2. Ernst Bloch, *Avicenna und die Aristotelische Linke* (Berlin: Rütten & Loening, 1952); Ernst Bloch, *Das Materialismusproblem: seine Geschichte und Substanz* (Frankfurt: Suhrkamp, 1972).
3. Ernst Bloch, *Gesamtausgabe* (Frankfurt: Suhrkamp, 1977), 7:479–546. Bloch describes the work's publication history in a letter to Peter Huchel, no. 8, in Ernst Bloch, *Briefe* (Frankfurt: Suhrkamp, 1985), 2:859.
4. Jordani Bruni Nolani [Giordano Bruno], *Opera Latine Conscripta*, trans. Francesco Fiorentino (Neapoli: D. Morano, 1879), 1.1.58–71.
5. Avicenna, *Die Metaphysik Avicennas, enthaltend die Metaphysik, Theologie, Kosmologie und Ethik*, trans. Max Horten (Halle an der Saale: Rudolf Haupt, 1907); Avicenna, *The Metaphysics of the Healing*, trans. Michael Marmura (Provo, UT: Brigham Young University Press, 2005).

INTRODUCTION

1. Ernst Bloch to Peter Huchel, no. 8, in Ernst Bloch, *Briefe* (Frankfurt: Suhrkamp, 1985), 2:858. Bloch uses both "Ibn Sina" and "Avicenna," and we follow him throughout.

2. See Robert Pasnau, introduction to *The Cambridge History of Medieval Philosophy*, rev. ed., ed. Robert Pasnau (Cambridge: Cambridge University Press, 2014), 1–8; Dimitri Gutas, "Origins in Baghdad," in Pasnau, *The Cambridge History of Medieval Philosophy*, 9–25.
3. For treatments of Bloch in English, see Vincent Geoghegan, *Ernst Bloch* (London: Routledge, 1996); Wayne Hudson, *The Marxist Philosophy of Ernst Bloch* (London: St. Martin's, 1982); Peter Thompson and Slavoj Žižek, eds., *The Privatization of Hope* (Durham, NC: Duke University Press, 2013). The literature in German is more extensive; see the indispensable volumes Unseld Siegried, ed., *Ernst Bloch zu Ehren: Beiträge zu seinem Werk* (Frankfurt: Suhrkamp, 1965); *Ernst Blochs Wirkung: ein Arbeitsbuch zum 90. Geburtstag* (Frankfurt: Suhrkamp 1975); Beat Dietschy, Doris Zeilinger, and Rainer Zimmermann, eds., *Bloch-Wörterbuch* (Berlin: De Gruyter, 2012).
4. Rolf Wiggershaus, *The Frankfurt School* (Cambridge, MA: MIT Press, 1994), 65, 69; Pierre Bouretz, *Witnesses for the Future* (Baltimore: Johns Hopkins University Press, 2010), 427.
5. That is, he lived in East Germany at first. Bloch defected to West Germany in 1961.
6. Ernst Bloch's works in English include *Man on His Own: Essays in the Philosophy of Religion*, trans. E. B. Ashton (New York: Herder & Herder, 1970); *A Philosophy of the Future*, trans John Cumming (New York: Herder & Herder, 1970); *Atheism in Christianity* (New York: Herder & Herder, 1972; London: Verso, 2009); *The Principle of Hope*, 3 vols. (Cambridge, MA: MIT Press, 1986); *Natural Law and Human Dignity*, trans. Dennis Schmidt (Cambridge, MA: MIT Press, 1987); *The Utopian Function of Art and Literature: Selected Essays*, trans. Jack Zipes and Frank Mecklenburg (Cambridge, MA: MIT Press, 1989); *The Heritage of Our Times*, trans. Neville and Steven Plaice (Oxford: Blackwell, 1991); *The Spirit of Utopia*, trans. Anthony A. Nassar (Stanford, CA: Stanford University Press, 2000); *Traces*, trans. Anthony A. Nassar (Stanford, CA: Stanford University Press, 2006); *On Karl Marx* (London: Verso, 2018). *Man on His Own* is a collection of essays, and *A Philosophy of the Future* is the first part of his Tübingen introductory lectures to philosophy. The main discussions of Bloch's materialism currently available in English are in *The Principle of Hope*, 2:686–91, 3:1354–76; the latter section comprises the bulk of *On Karl Marx*.
7. See Theodor Adorno, "Blochs *Spuren*" (originally "*Grosse Blochmusik*"), in *Noten zur Literatur* (Frankfurt: Suhrkamp, 2002), 233–50; Detlev Claussen, *Theodor W. Adorno: One Last Genius*, trans. Rodney Livingstone (Cambridge, MA: Harvard University Press, 2008), 408n244; on Nostradamus, see Bouretz, *Witnesses for the Future*, 427.

8. Jürgen Habermas, "Ernst Bloch: A Marxist Schelling," in *Philosophical-Political Profiles*, trans. Frederick G. Lawrence (Cambridge, MA: MIT Press, 1983), 66.
9. George M. Logan and Robert M. Adams, introduction to *Utopia*, by Thomas More (Cambridge: Cambridge University Press, 1989), ix.
10. Hope is one of Christianity's three theological virtues alongside faith and love; see 1 Corinthians 13:13.
11. Hesiod, *Works and Days*, in *Hesiod and Theognis*, trans. Dorothea Wender (London: Penguin, 1973), ll. 93–99.
12. See Bloch, *The Principle of Hope*, chaps. 43–55.
13. See Johan Siebers, "Novum," in *Bloch-Wörterbuch*, 633–64.
14. Ernst Bloch, *Das Prinzip Hoffnung* (Frankfurt: Suhrkamp, 1977), *Gesamtausgabe* 5:728; Bloch, *The Principle of Hope*, 2:624; Bloch's emphasis.
15. Bloch, *Das Materialismusproblem*, in *Gesamtausgabe* 7:469.
16. Bloch, *Das Prinzip Hoffnung*, 5:1.
17. See Bloch, *The Principle of Hope*, chap. 18.
18. Bloch, *The Principle of Hope*, 1:198.
19. It is significant that Bloch saw his work on materialism as preparatory for his later work *The Principle of Hope*. See Sylvia Markun, *Ernst Bloch* (Berlin: Rohwohlt, 1977), 60ff.
20. See Frederick C. Beiser, "The Materialism Controversy," chap. 2 of *After Hegel: German Philosophy, 1840–1900* (Princeton: Princeton University Press, 2014). For the longer story, see Frederick C. Beiser, *The Fate of Reason* (Cambridge, MA: Harvard University Press, 1987).
21. See Frederick Engels, *Anti-Dühring* (1878; Moscow: Progress, 1969); Frederick Engels, *Dialectics of Nature* (1883; Moscow: Progress, 1964); Vladimir I. Lenin, *Materialism and Empirio-Criticism* (1909), in *Lenin: Collected Works* (Moscow: Progress, 1972), vol. 14.
22. Karl Marx, "Theses on Feuerbach," in *Karl Marx: Selected Writings*, ed. David McLellan (Oxford: Oxford University Press, 1977), 156.
23. Karl Marx, *Economic and Philosophic Manuscripts*, in *Karl Marx: Selected Writings*, 90.
24. Bloch, *The Principle of Hope*, 2:686–91.
25. Marx, *Economic and Philosophical Manuscripts*, 83.
26. Bloch, *The Principle of Hope*, 1:197.
27. Ernst Bloch, "Something's Missing," in *The Utopian Function of Art and Literature*, 12.
28. Bloch, *The Principle of Hope*, 1:198.
29. Bloch, *The Principle of Hope*, 1:197.

30. For analyses of the relevant sections of Aristotle, see Aristotle, *Metaphysics: Books Z and H*, trans. David Bostock (Oxford: Clarendon, 1994); Aristotle, *Metaphysics: Book Θ*, trans. Stephen Makin (Oxford: Clarendon, 2006).
31. Aristotle, 1032b1–2.
32. See Aristotle, 1045b17ff. Makin notes that a better translation of *dynamis* is "power" rather than the standard "potentiality"; see Aristotle, 1045b22.
33. In addition to books Z, H, and Θ of Aristotle's *Metaphysics*, see also book Δ, chap. 12.
34. For an exposition of Bloch that stresses his "open system," see Hudson, *The Marxist Philosophy of Ernst Bloch*.
35. Aristotle, *Metaphysics* 1048b29; Ernst Bloch, *Tendenz, Latenz, Utopie* (Frankfurt: Suhrkamp, 1978), 409.
36. Bloch, *The Principle of Hope*, 1:209.
37. Bloch, *The Principle of* Hope, 1:209; translation emended.
38. Bloch to Horkheimer, 10 September 1936, in Bloch, *Briefe*, 2:676–77. Had Horkheimer and Theodor Adorno been more forgiving in their assessment of Bloch's efforts—they were unhappy that his study didn't cite their work—and agreed to publish it, Bloch's materialism might be better known today. See Horkheimer to Adorno, 26 September 1937, Theodor Adorno and Max Horkheimer, *Briefe und Briefwechsel*, vol. 1, *1928–1940* (Frankfurt: Suhrkamp, 1994), 415; Adorno to Bloch, 2 October 1937, Adorno and Horkheimer, *Briefe und Briefwechsel*, 539. Jean-Baptiste Robinet is the only name Bloch mentions in his letter that does not appear in *Avicenna and the Aristotelian Left*; he does, however, appear in *Das Materialismusproblem*, 7:186, 201.
39. See, e.g., Theodor Adorno, "On the Fetish Character in Music and Regression in Listening," in *The Essential Frankfurt School Reader*, ed. Andrew Arato and Eike Gebhardt (New York: Continuum, 1994), 270–99; Theodor Adorno, *Aesthetic Theory*, trans. Robert Hullot-Kentor (Minneapolis: University of Minnesota Press, 1997); Herbert Marcuse, *One-Dimensional Man* (Boston: Beacon, 1964), 256ff.; Herbert Marcuse, *The Aesthetic Dimension* (Boston: Beacon, 1979).
40. Bloch, *The Principle of Hope*, 1:214–15, cf. 249; Werner Jung, "Vor-Schein," in Dietschy, Zeilinger, and Zimmermann, *Bloch-Wörterbuch*, 664–72.
41. Readers interested in more self-consciously scholarly treatments should look to Amos Bertolacci, *The Reception of Aristotle's Metaphysics in Avicenna's Kitāb al-Šifā* (Leiden: Brill, 2006); Jon McGinnis, *Avicenna* (Oxford: Oxford University Press, 2010); Dimitri Gutas, *Avicenna and the Aristotelian Tradition*, 2nd ed. (Leiden: Brill, 2014).
42. See Bloch, *The Heritage of Our Times*, 97–116.

43. On gloss traditions, see John Marenbon, "The Emergence of Medieval Latin Philosophy," in Pasnau, *The Cambridge History of Medieval Philosophy*, 1:33.
44. See p. 18 in this text.
45. This is meant as a rough and by no means definitive categorization of new materialisms in current political theory. Jane Bennett, *Vibrant Matter* (Durham, NC: Duke University Press, 2010); William Connolly, *A World of Becoming* (Durham, NC: Duke University Press, 2010); Graham Harman, *Tool-Being: Heidegger and the Metaphysics of Objects* (Chicago: Open Court, 2002); Timothy Morton, *The Ecological Thought* (Cambridge, MA: Harvard University Press, 2010); Bruno Latour, "On Actor-Network Theory: A Few Clarifications," *Soziale Welt* 47, no 4 (1996): 369–81; Manuel Delanda, *A New Philosophy of Society* (New York: Bloomsbury, 2006).
46. Louis Althusser, "The Underground Current of the Materialism of the Encounter," in *Philosophy of the Encounter*, ed. Oliver Corpet and Francois Matheron, trans. G. M. Goshgarian (London: Verso, 2006), 163–207; Louis Althusser, *Machiavelli and Us* (London: Verso, 1999).
47. Ilya Prigogine and Isabelle Stengers, *Order Out of Chaos* (Toronto: Bantam, 1984), 9.
48. Alfred Schmidt, *The Concept of Nature in Marx*, trans. Ben Fowkes (London: New Left, 1971), 161. Jürgen Habermas offers a similar critique in "Ernst Bloch: A Marxist Schelling."
49. See Bloch, *Briefe*, 2:818–19.

AVICENNA AND THE ARISTOTELIAN LEFT

Epigraph: "The drawing of forms out of matter." This is not a quote from Avicenna or Averroës but a pithy statement of the eduction theory of form-matter; the relevant source is *Ibn Rushd's Metaphysics*, trans. C. Genenquand (1499; Leiden: Brill, 1984), 109; see also below, 23, 67. Bloch added this epigraph to the Suhrkamp edition; in the first monograph edition published by Rütten and Loening, an aphorism by Leonardo da Vinci is used as the epigraph instead: "He who fixes his course by a star changes not."

1. Bloch's use of the Arabic "Ibn Sina" and the Latin "Avicenna" is followed throughout.
2. Present-day Uzbekistan. For a map of Avicenna's world, see Jon McGinnis, *Avicenna* (Oxford: Oxford University Press, 2010), 5; see the rest of McGinnis's chapter 1 for Avicenna's life and intellectual milieu, which is more reliable than the biography Bloch offers, the flaws of which are

remarked on in the following notes. For the text of Avicenna's "Autobiography," see Dimitri Gutas, *Avicenna and the Aristotelian Tradition*, 2nd ed. (Leiden: Brill, 2014), 10–19.
3. Bloch's incorrect reference to Avicenna studying at the "University of Baghdad" has been removed. There was not a university as such in Baghdad at the time, nor did Avicenna train in that city.
4. Present-day Iran.
5. This sentence replaces Bloch's incorrect reference to healing the "son of the caliph of Baghdad"; in fact, he advised court physicians in the treatment of Nuh ibn-Mansur. He did not, moreover, obtain great wealth and led a fairly unstable and peripatetic life.
6. "Between 40 and 275 titles have been attributed to [Avicenna] by bibliographers, ... with approximately 130 reckoned to be authentic." Robert Wisnovsky, "Avicenna and the Avicennian Tradition," in *The Cambridge Companion to Arabic Philosophy*, ed. Peter Adamson and Richard C. Taylor (Cambridge: Cambridge University Press, 2005), 92; for further discussion, see appendix in Gutas, *Avicenna and the Aristotelian Tradition*.
7. Eighty-seven translations of this work were made in medieval Europe. See Parviz Morewedge, foreword to *The Metaphysics of Avicenna (Ibn Sina)* (New York: Columbia University Press, 1973), xv.
8. **Bloch's note: See Bogutdinow on this in the Soviet journal *Woprosy Philosophii* [*Problems of Philosophy*] 3/1948, p. 358ff.** A. M. Bogoutdinov, "An Outstanding Document of Tadjik Philosophic Thought," 358–66, as cited in J. Miller and M. Miller, "*Voprosy Filosofi* (*Problems of Philosophy*), 3 (1948)," *Soviet Studies* 1, no. 3 (January 1950): 210–30, which summarizes the article on pp. 225–26.
9. Bloch presumably means Iran's Association for the Defense of Peace, Solidarity, and Democracy, a member of the World Peace Council; on the WPC, see Lawrence Wittner, *One World or None: A History of the World Nuclear Disarmament Movement Through 1953* (Stanford, CA: Stanford University Press, 1993), 184–86.
10. *Avicenna and the Aristotelian Left* appeared in 1952, coinciding with the commemoration Bloch describes, during which the Hamadan mausoleum now housing Avicenna's grave was dedicated.
11. "Fitting": *fällig*, also meaning "due," as in birth.
12. "Those fixated on the beyond": *Die Jenseitigen*.
13. Present-day Jordan and Syria, respectively.
14. This refers to CE 636; Muhammad died in CE 632.
15. *Cum grano salis*: "with a grain of salt."

16. This refers to CE 622, when Muhammad left Mecca for Medina and the Islamic calendar commences.
17. As Bloch well knows, the legendary Sinbad the Sailor was a merchant. See *Tales from the Thousand and One Nights*, ed. W. Harvey (New York: Penguin, 1973), 113–62.
18. "Land of the Franks"; Bloch employs this medieval Persian metonym for the West to express the latter's peripheral status to the Middle East's commercial and intellectual centers of the early Middle Ages.
19. Iamblichus (ca. CE 245–ca. 325).
20. This is a reference to the cult of Mithra, the ancient Persian god of light, subsequently revived in the Mithraic Mysteries cult of the Roman Empire. As Bloch explains, a central tenet of Neoplatonism was that Being emanated downward from the divine, often represented as light; for this idea in Christian Neoplatonism, see Pseudo-Dionysius, *The Divine Names*, in *Pseudo-Dionysius: The Complete Works*, trans. Paul Rorem (New York: Paulist Press, 1987), 74 (697c).
21. Chosroes I ruled from CE 531 to 579; in 529, Christian Roman emperor Justinian (ruling CE 527–565) closed the Neoplatonist Academy in a bid to suppress paganism. Damascius, its last scholarch, fled with his associates to Chosroes's court in Persia.
22. Abu Jafar Abdullah ibn Muhammad al Mansur (714–775) was the second Abbasid caliph.
23. Roger Bacon (ca. 1214–ca. 1292) was an English natural philosopher; Albertus Magnus (ca. 1200–1280) was a German philosopher and theologian.
24. It is worth noting that Bacon's *scientia experimentalis* is broader than the concept of modern scientific experiment under controlled laboratory conditions, as the Latin connotes knowledge through experience, not necessarily through investigation.
25. See Alexander von Humboldt, *Cosmos*, trans. E. C. Otté (London: Longman, Brown, Green and Longmans, 1849), 2:213.
26. See Pseudo-Dionysius, *The Divine Names*, 50 (588c).
27. *Glauben* means both "faith" and "belief"; "faith" is a better translation in this context, but the ambiguity should be kept in mind.
28. "Precursor of Christ."
29. Anselm of Canterbury (ca. 1033–1109) was an English theologian and author of the best-known version of the ontological argument discussed further on. Thomas Aquinas (1225–1274) was an Italian philosopher and theologian.
30. John Scotus Eriugena (ca. 815–ca. 877) was an Irish philosopher and theologian.

31. "Truth of reason," "truth of authority," and "to determine the rules of true religion," respectively.
32. 1 Corinthians 3:19.
33. Tertullian (ca. CE 155–ca. 240) was an early Christian apologist; see his "On the Flesh of Christ," sec. 5, para. 4. The Latin literally reads, "I believe because it is absurd, because it is impossible."
34. "Pulled away from": *abtrieb*, from the verb *abtreiben*, which also means "to abort."
35. *Fremdartigerweise* also means "in a foreign way."
36. The Albigensians, also known as Cathars, were a radically anticlerical sect with a particularly significant following in twelfth-century Languedoc, and they became the target of a papal crusade beginning in 1209; see Joseph Strayer, *The Albigensian Crusades* (New York: Oxford University Press, 1970); Emmanuel Le Roy Ladurie, *Montaillou*, trans. Barbara Bray (New York: Penguin, 1990). Meister Eckhart (ca. 1260–1328), or Eckhart von Hochheim, was a German Christian mystic.
37. Gnosticism includes a variety of mystical, emanationist, and antimaterialist writings composed in the first centuries of Christianity, often in conversation with and even self-identifying as Christian. The classic popular discussion is Elaine Pagels, *The Gnostic Gospels* (New York: Vintage, 1979). For a discussion of emanation in Avicenna's interpretation of Aristotle, see Herbert A. Davidson, *Alfarabi, Avicenna, and Averroës, on Intellect* (New York: Oxford University Press, 1992), chap. 4.
38. This parenthetical expression means that even great minds make mistakes. See Horace, *Ars poetica* l. 359: "quandoque bonus dormitat Homerus."
39. See Avicenne, *Réfutation de l'Astrologie*, trans. Y. Michot (Beyrouth: Les Éditions Albouraq, 2006).
40. On the Brethren of Purity, see Richard Ian Netton, *Muslim Neoplatonists: An Introduction to the Thought of the Brethren of Purity* (London: Routledge, 2002); more specifically on the point at hand, see Carmela Baffioni, "Metaphors of Light and the 'Verse of Light' in the Brethren of Purity," in *In the Age of al-Farabi*, ed. Peter Adamson (London/Turin: Warburg Institute—Nino Aragno Editore, 2008), 163–77.
41. "Church" is translated from *Kirche*; "mosque" makes more metonymic sense, but we follow Bloch's text.
42. "Pneumatic" truth is spiritual, nonmaterial truth. See Bloch's discussion of Origen's hermeneutics further on here.
43. Abū-Sa'īd Abul-Khayr (967–1049) was a Persian Sufi. This quatrain has been translated from the Persian by Jamal Elias; for the original, see *Sukhanān-i manẓum-i Abu Sa'id-i Abu'l-Khayr*, ed. Sa'id Nafisi (Tehran:

Intishārāt-i Kitābkhāna-yi Shams, 1955), 41, ruba'i 281. A rhyming translation can be found in Mahmood Jamal, ed. and trans., *Islamic Mystical Poetry: Sufi Verse from the Early Mystics to Rumi* (London: Penguin, 2009), 36.

44. **Bloch's note: Ignác Goldziher, *Vorlesungen über den Islam*, [Heidelberg, C. Winter,] 1910, 172.** Like Horten, Goldziher, who was Bloch's other principal source on Islam, belongs to an early generation of Orientalists; see the critical discussion of his work in Edward Said, *Orientalism* (New York: Vintage, 1979), 209. That said, Bloch directs his harshest words at Horten; see his note here (note 62).
45. "Skipping over": *überspringung*, "sublation": *aufhebung*.
46. See Gottfried Ephraim Lessing, *Nathan the Wise*, in *"Nathan the Wise," "Minna von Barnhelm," and Other Plays and Writings*, ed. Peter Demetz (New York: Continuum, 1991), 173–276. See Giovanni Boccaccio, *The Decameron*, trans. G. H. McWilliam (New York: Penguin, 1995), 41–43.
47. *De Tribus Impostoribus* was a legendary antireligious tract rumored to exist in late Middle Ages, and an ostensible (hoax) copy of it was published in 1712 with the title *La Vie et l'Esprit de M. Benoit Spinoza*, which was subsequently republished in 1719 with the new title *Traité des Trois Imposteurs*. Another version entitled *De Tribus Impostoribus* was published in 1753 with the false publication date of 1598, presumably written by the German jurist Johan Joachim Müller. See Georges Minois, *Le Traité des Trois Imposteurs: Histoire d'un livre blasphématoire qui n'existait pas* (Paris: Albin Michel, 2009); on the context in which Bloch invokes this work, see Patrick Marcolini, "Le *De Tribus Impostoribus* (*Traité des 3 imposteurs*) et les origines arabes de l'athéisme philosophique européen," *Les Cahiers de l'ATP* (October 2003). On the relationship between Frederick II (1194–1250) and the fable of the three imposters, see Steven Runciman, *A History of the Crusades* (Cambridge: Cambridge University Press, 1987), 3:190; we have modified Bloch's reference to "Frederick the Great" so as to avoid confusion with his more famous namesake, the much later King of Prussia (1712–1786).
48. Joachim of Fiore (1135–1202) was an Italian theologian. On his doctrine of the three ages of man, see Marjorie Reeves, *Joachim of Fiore and the Prophetic Future* (New York: Sutton, 1999), 1–22.
49. On the Brothers of the Free Spirit, see Norman R. Cohn, *The Pursuit of the Millennium* (New York: Oxford, 1970), chap. 8.
50. Abū Ḥāmid Muḥammad ibn Muḥammad al-Ghazālī (ca. 1058–1111) was a Persian antirationalist philosopher and theologian. See his *The Incoherence of the Philosophers*, trans. Michael Marmura, 2nd ed. (Provo, UT: Brigham Young University Press, 2002).

51. Bloch cites Ibn Tufayl, who cites Ghazālī; see *Ibn Tufayl's Hayy Ibn Yaqzan: A Philosophical Tale*, trans. Lenn Goodman (Chicago: University of Chicago Press, 2009), 101, where this is poetically translated: "Forget all you've heard and clutch what you see— / at sunrise what use is Saturn to thee?"
52. Origen (CE 185–254) was an early Christian theologian. Pseudo-Dionysius continued this tradition of allegorism; see, e.g., *The Celestial Hierarchy* chap. 15; *The Ecclesiastical Hierarchy* 373b.
53. "To transcend": *aufzuheben*.
54. See note 51 here. Jim Colville writes that a more accurate English title would be "A Living Son of Consciousness"; see Jim Colville, introduction to *Two Andalusian Philosophers* (London: Kegan Paul, 1999), vii.
55. Avicenna's allegory of Hayy ibn Yaqzan can be found in Henry Corbin, *Avicenna and the Visionary Recital* (Princeton: Princeton University Press, 1960), 137–50.
56. The titles translate as *The Self-Taught Philosopher* and *The Natural Human* respectively. See Ibn Tufayl, *Philosophus Autodidactus, sive, Epistola Abi Jaafar ebn Tophail de Hai ebn Yokdhan* (Oxford: H. Hall, 1671); Ibn Tufayl, *Naturmensch, oder Geschichte des Hai Ebn Joktan: Ein morgenländischer Roman* (Berlin and Stettin: F. Nicolai, 1783). Bloch's sentence structure here is particularly unusual; we have reconstructed his meaning the best we can.
57. "Mystical union."
58. *Ibn Tufayl's Hayy ibn Yaqzan*, 96–97. "His" at the beginning of the passage refers to a Sufi devotee. This translation is slightly amended with reference to Colville's rendering: Colville, introduction, 4–5; see note 54 here. Bloch cites Ibn Tufayl, *Der Naturmensch*, 30ff.
59. Averroës invokes Alexander of Aphrodisias; see Averroës, *Tahafut al-Tahafut (The Incoherence of the Incoherence)*, trans. Simon van den Bergh (London: Luzac, 1954), 253–54. Bloch cites Horten's translation in Averroës, *Die Hauptlehren des Averroës nach seiner Schrift; Die Widerlegung des Gazali*, trans. Max Horten (Bonn: Marcus and Weber Verlag, 1913), 234. Alexander of Aphrodisias (fl. CE 200) was a Greek Peripatetic philosopher.
60. "Body of heaven."
61. "This World" in heading: *Diesseits*.
62. **Bloch's Note: It should not be forgotten that the earlier Catholic theologian M. Horten, someone without much of an elective affinity for enlightened matter, when translating and glossing Avicenna and Averroës, wrote them off as mere "enlighteners." Their naturalism was to be seen as nothing more than a "primitive misunderstanding of Scholasticism," apparently supported by inadequate Latin translations. In Horten we are surprised to find, for example, that Averroës is turned from an**

antiorthodox thinker into an "apologist for the Qur'an." This makes it difficult, of course, for Horten to accuse him of the "tendency toward pantheism," which he also claims to have found. It is a shame that the Islamic orthodoxy of that time, which persecuted Avicenna and Averroës and burned their books, was not itself true to the Qur'an and, on the contrary, saw reading it merely as a matter of lip service. Alas, this clergy took the naturalism in both philosophers more literally than does a reactionary Arabist today, *post festum* ["after the fact"]. And as far as the distinctly subversive effect of Averroëism in the Christian Middle Ages is concerned, then, its "primitive misunderstanding" does not appear to lie in its Scholasticism, whose least serious mistake was primitiveness. No, Averroës and Avicenna still stand firm against the world of the mufti and his orthodoxy, and to wish to retrospectively assimilate them is not scholarly work but confabulation.

63. Georg Wilhelm Friedrich Hegel's adherents fell into "Left" and "Right" camps that emphasized progressive and conservative elements of his thought, respectively. Left Hegelians stressed the incomplete realization of history's telos as the idea of freedom as well as the capacity of humans to deliberately contribute to this development and largely supported reformist or revolutionary politics. Right Hegelians stressed the supposed inherent rationality of existing social formations and the relative impotence of intentional human agency against the transhistorical "cunning of reason" and tended to support statism and conservative politics. See John Toews, *Hegelianism* (Cambridge: Cambridge University Press, 1980); Warren Breckman, *Marx, the Young Hegelians, and the Origins of Radical Social Theory* (Cambridge: Cambridge University Press, 1998); Douglas Moggach, ed., *The New Hegelians* (Cambridge: Cambridge University Press, 2006). For important Left Hegelian writings, see L. Stepelevich, ed., *The Young Hegelians: An Anthology* (Cambridge: Cambridge University Press, 1997).

64. Bloch rendered this as *In-Möglichkeit-Sein*. On Bloch's categories of *In-Möglichkeit-Sein* and *Nach-Möglichkeit-Sein*, or "what-may-become-possible" and "what-is-considered-possible," see the introduction.

65. "Actively effective thing": *aktiv Wirksame*.

66. Aquinas defined God as "pure act"; see, e.g., Thomas Aquinas, "God Is His Essence," chap. 10 in *Compendium of Theology*, trans. Richard J. Regan (Oxford: Oxford University Press, 2009), 22–23.

67. Strato of Lampsacus (BCE ca. 335–ca. 269) was a Greek philosopher.

68. Avicebron, or Solomon ibn Gabirol (ca. 1022–1070), was an Andalusian Jewish philosopher and poet.

69. *Natura naturans,* or "nature naturing," is a self-causing activity, in contrast to *natura naturata,* or "nature [having been] natured," which is the passive product of mechanistic causality. The concept is today most associated with Benedict de Spinoza; see Bloch's discussion of *deus sive natura* further on.
70. Giordano Bruno (1548–1600) was an Italian philosopher and humanist who was burned at the stake for heresy.
71. "Universal life": *All-Leben.*
72. "Sublation": *Aufhebung.*
73. *In-Möglichkeit-Sein.*
74. "Stick" is translated from *Peitsche.* The phrase *Mit Zuckerbrot und Peitsche* (literally, "with sugarbread and whip") is equivalent to the English "carrot and stick," and hence the terms have been so translated here.
75. Aristotle's *nous* has been variously rendered as "mind," "spirit," "intellect," and more. In this section, Bloch uses the Kantian-Hegelian language of *Verstand* (understanding) and *Vernunft* (reason); elsewhere he employs the Scholastic language of *Intelligenz* (intelligence).
76. *Habitus* is Aquinas's term for Aristotle's *hexis* (ἕξις), meaning "active character" or "disposition." See Robert C. Miner, "Aquinas on Habitus," in *A History of Habit: from Aristotle to Bourdieu,* ed. T. Sparrow and A. Hutchinson (New York: Lexington, 2013), 67–88.
77. This is translated from Bloch's German. Cf. Averroës, *Long Commentary on Aristotle's De Anima,* ed. F. S. Crawford (Cambridge. MA: Medieval Academy of America, 1953), 433.
78. See Averroës, *On Aristotle's "Metaphysics": An Annotated Translation of the So-Called "Epitome,"* ed. Rüdiger Arnzen (Berlin: De Gruyter, 2010), 169.
79. The Kabbalah posits ten *sephirot* (סְפִירוֹת), or basic emanations of the infinite. The classic (pagan) systematic account of Neoplatonist metaphysics is Proclus, *The Elements of Theology,* 2nd ed., trans. E. R. Dodds (Oxford: Clarendon, 1992); the influential Christian account of the same is by Pseudo-Dionysius the Areopagite in *The Complete Works* (New York: Paulist Press, 1987). For emanationism, see, e.g., Pseudo-Dionysius, *The Divine Names* 649b.
80. See Avicenna, *The Metaphysics of the Healing,* trans. Michael Marmura (Provo, UT: Brigham Young University Press, 2005), 325–26; cf. Davidson, *Alfarabi, Avicenna, and Averroës,* 76.
81. This is the doctrine of ἔννοια, translated by Cicero as *notitia* and *intelligentia,* and which he described as being "imprinted" on all minds through the senses. See Henry Dyson, *Prolepsis and Ennoia in the Early Stoa* (Berlin: De Gruyter, 2009), xvi, appendix C6, C3. See also R. J. Hankinson, "Stoic Epistemology," in *The Cambridge Companion to Stoicism,* ed. Brad Inwood

(Cambridge: Cambridge University Press, 2003), 59–84. See also the texts in A. A. Long and D. N. Sedley, *The Hellenistic Philosophers* (Cambridge: Cambridge University Press, 1987), 1:39–42.

82. Matthew 16:19.
83. "On the Unity of the Intellect against the Averroists." Albertus Magnus and his student Thomas Aquinas both wrote works against Averroism. Albertus's *De Unitate Intellectus Contra Averroem* was commissioned by Pope Alexander VI in 1256, and Aquinas's better-known *De Unitate Intellectus contra Averroistas* dates from 1270. See Beatrice Zedler, introduction to *On the Unity of the Intellect Against the Averroists*, by Thomas Aquinas (Milwaukee: Marquette University Press, 1968), 4. The standard edition of this work is now *Aquinas Against the Averroists*, trans. Ralph McInerny (West Lafayette, IN: Purdue University Press, 1993).
84. The moniker "Poor Conrad" was given to several secret peasants' leagues, which, in 1514, revolted against the Duke of Württemberg and other nobles; see Andreas Schmauder, "Der Arme Konrad in Württemberg und im badischen Bühl," in *Bundschuh: Untergrombach 1502, das unruhige Reich und die Revolutionierbarkeit Europas*, ed. P. Blickle and T. Adam (Stuttgart: Franz Steiner Verlag, 2004), 183–94. Pentecost, or Shavuot, celebrates the giving of the Torah to the people of Israel, hence the materialization of the divine spirit.
85. Thomas Münzer (ca. 1489–1525) was a German theologian and a key figure in the 1525 peasant uprising, about whom Bloch wrote *Thomas Münzer als Theologe der Revolution*, vol. 2 of *Gesamtausgabe* (Frankfurt: Suhrkamp, 1969), cf. 45.
86. "Active or universal intellect."
87. *In-Möglichkeit-Sein*.
88. In contradistinction to "prime" or "first" matter.
89. *Nach-Möglichkeit-Sein*.
90. The German parenthetical comment is similarly awkward: "wenn auch, wie eben in der gestalteten Weltmaterie, eine gegebenenfalls selber negative mitverursachende, eine sine qua non." In other words, in Aristotle matter is the passive element of the form/matter collaboration, the substance in which active form realizes latent potential.
91. Bloch's reference here reads **Physics, chap. 5**; it appears that he means book H, chap. 5. For unfinished entelechy, see also Aristotle, *Physics* 202b30–33; Aristotle, *Metaphysics* 1049b18–34, 1066a20–23, and this translation's introduction. Cf. Franz Brentano, *The Theory of Categories*, trans. Roderick Chisholm and Norbert Guterman (1907; The Hague: Martinus Nijhoff, 1981), 58–62.

92. See, e.g., Avicenna, *The Metaphysics of the Healing*, 30 (1.6).
93. For Bloch, *Das* (that) describes bare existence, while *Was* (what) describes existence with meaningful content. See, e.g., Ernst Bloch, *Experimentum Mundi*, in *Gesamtausgabe*, 15:31. In his philosophical anthropology, humans are always in search of a "what."
94. "Fiat" is given in Latin, meaning "let it be done."
95. Avicenna, *The Metaphysics of the Healing*, 335–36. The passage Bloch cites from the German translation, Avicenna, *Die Metaphysik Avicennas, enthaltend die Metaphysik, Theologie, Kosmologie, und Ethik*, trans. Max Horten (Halle a.S.: R. Haupt, 1907; Frankfurt: Minerva, 1960), 611–12, differs slightly from Marmura's English translation, possibly because they follow different Avicennian manuscript traditions; see note 198 here.
96. Bloch's phrasing here has been modified for comprehension; thanks to Jon McGinnis for his helpful suggestions.
97. "Active-Actuality": *Wirk-Wirklichkeit*. *Wirken* means, among many other things, "to effectuate" and "to operate," and *Wirklichkeit* means "reality" or "actuality." Bloch intends his term to convey the capacity for self-realizing potentiality. Because *wirk-* is polysemous and repetition is the most notable feature of Bloch's clumsy neologism, we have opted for "Active-Actuality."
98. Neither of these specific phrases seems to be in Avicenna, whose treatment of the four elements can be found in his *Physics* 2.3 and passim. For further discussion, see Anneliese Maier, *An der Grenze von Scholastik und Naturwissenschaft* (Rome: Edizioni di Storia e Letteratura, 1952), 22–36.
99. This does not appear to be a direct quote from Averroës but rather is the basic principle of Aristotelian-cum-Averroean celestial dynamics; see Aristotle, *On the Heavens*, in *The Complete Works of Aristotle*, ed. J. Barnes (Princeton: Princeton University Press, 1984), 447–511; cf. Averroës, *De Substantia Orbis*, trans. Arthur Hyman (Cambridge, MA: Medieval Academy of America, 1986), esp. 77–79. In Avicenna's and Averroës's cosmologies, a "fiery orbit" exists between the outermost sphere of fixed stars and the subordinate orbits of air, water, and earth; see Majid Fakhry, *Averroës (Ibn Rushd)* (Oxford: One World, 2008), 53.
100. **Bloch's Note: "First Discussion."**
101. "Nature supernaturing" and "nature supernatured," respectively; in other words, material nature creating the supernatural.
102. See Avicenna, *Metaphysics of the Healing*, 7 (1.2).
103. William of Ockham (ca. 1287–1347) was an English philosopher.
104. "Inherent forms" and "separate forms" respectively.

105. The exclamation point is Bloch's addition, drawing attention to *ita*, "therefore."
106. Translated from Bloch's German. Cf. Thomas Aquinas, *Summa Theologica* (New York: Benziger, 1948), 20 (1.4.a.1): "For since matter as such is merely potential, the first material principle must be simply potential, and thus most imperfect."
107. Arius (ca. CE 250–336) was an early Christian presbyter; Sabellius (fl. ca. 215) was an early Christian theologian. The fresco is *The Triumph of Saint Thomas Aquinas*, now attributed to Andrea di Bonaiuto da Firenze.
108. See Johann Wolfgang von Goethe, *Faust, Part I*, trans. David Constantine (London: Penguin, 2005), l:461. For a reading of *Faust* as a harbinger of capitalist modernity, see Marshall Berman, *All That Is Solid Melts Into Air* (New York: Verso, 2010), chap. 1.
109. Siger of Brabant (ca. 1240–1284) was a Low Countries philosopher.
110. Moshe ben Maimon (ca. 1135–1204) was an Arabic Jewish philosopher.
111. *Suum quique*: "may all get their due."
112. *Lumen natural*: "natural light." We replace *Proportion* with *Proposition*, which was almost certainly Bloch's intended word.
113. Alexander of Hales (ca. 1185–1245) was an English theologian and philosopher.
114. Aristotle distinguished four "causes," the sum of which explain a particular thing's existence: (1) material, that out of which the thing is composed; (2) formal, the archetype of the fully realized thing toward which it develops; (3) efficient, or the force that brings about the thing's realization; and (4) final, or the purpose for which the thing exists. See Aristotle, *Physics* 2.3; cf. Avicenna, *The Physics of the Healing*, trans. Jon McGinnis (Provo, UT: Brigham Young University, 2009), 1:10.
115. **Bloch's note: Most decisively in Thomas's work on God the *creator*: *De ente et essentia*.** See Joseph Bobik, ed., *Aquinas on Being and Essence* (South Bend, IN: University of Notre Dame Press, 1965).
116. "Assumes": *aufhebt*.
117. *Naturierendes, also Schaffendes einer natura naturans*. The following clause has been slightly emended for clarity.
118. *Dies total Wirkliches*.
119. **Bloch's note: Just as according to Aquinas, in his worldly *analogia entis*, it is only actual warmth, like fire, that makes it possible for wood to achieve its potential of becoming warm in actuality.** See *Summa Theologica* 1.2.3.
120. This is translated from Bloch's German. Cf. Bobik, *Aquinas on Being and Essence*: "His essence is not other than his existence" (213).

121. Often translated as "I am who I am," Bloch is suggesting that אֶהְיֶה אֲשֶׁר אֶהְיֶה is better rendered by the futural, "I will be who [or what] I will be." "I am He . . ." is translated from Bloch's German. See Aquinas, *Summa Theologica* 1.13.11.
122. "Because God is the perfect being, he must be a real being." The classic version of the ontological proof can be found in Anselm, *Proslogion*, trans. T. Williams (Indianapolis: Hackett, 2001).
123. For Aquinas's "argument from contingency," a version of the cosmological argument building on Aristotle, see Aquinas, *Summa Theologica* 1.2.3.
124. *Humanitas*: "the quality of being a human," and *stellaritas*: "the quality of being a star."
125. The *mutakallim*, "students of *kalam*," that is, students of the revealed word, defend Islam against skeptics and unbelievers. See Oliver Leaman and Sajjad Rizvi, "The Developed *Kalam* Tradition," in *The Cambridge Companion to Classical Islamic Theology*, ed. Tim Winter (Cambridge: Cambridge University Press, 2008), 77–98. On the particular *mutakallim* with whom Avicenna and Averroës clashed, see Wisnovsky, "Avicenna and the Avicennian Tradition," 112ff.; Michael E. Marmura, "Avicenna and the *Kalam*," in *Probing in Islamic Philosophy* (Binghamton: SUNY Press, 2005), 95–130.
126. **Bloch's note: This is the term the Stoics gave to *energeia*, which they saw as productive divine reason within things.** See, e.g., Marcus Aurelius's reference to "Seminal Reason" in *Meditations*, in *Marcus Aurelius*, trans. C. R. Haines (Cambridge, MA: Harvard Loeb Library, 1916), 79 (4.21).
127. *Sich selber ausgebärende Materie.*
128. Goethe, *Faust, Part I*, l:384. Stuart Atkins translates *Wirkenskraft und Samen* as "seminal forces"; see J. W. von Goethe, *Faust I & II: Goethe's Collected Works*, trans. Stuart Atkins (Princeton: Princeton University Press, 2014).
129. See Guillaume de Lorris and Jean de Meun, *The Romance of the Rose*, trans. F. Horgan (Oxford: Oxford University Press, 1994).
130. See note 98 here.
131. Bloch's text reads, "John of Padua." There are several notable Johns of Padua, but all are considerably later; it is almost certain he means John of Jandun (ca. 1285–1323), a French Averroist who wrote on individuation and worked with Marsilius of Padua. Pietro d'Abano (ca. 1257–1316) was an Italian natural philosopher.
132. Amalric of Bena (d. ca. 1204–1207) was a French theologian; David of Dinant (ca. 1160–ca. 1217) was a French philosopher associated with Amalric.
133. "[He] most stupidly taught that God is prime matter." See Aquinas, *Summa Theologica* 1.3.8. Aquinas follows this comment with the explanation that

this is "manifest untruth; since it is not possible for God to enter into the composition of anything, either as a formal or a material principle."
134. We replace Bloch's "body" (*Körper*) with "spirit" to parallel the preceding sentence.
135. With his repeated use of the word *Kontakt*, "contact," Bloch makes a Hegelian move, saying, in effect, that David of Dinant's ideas were only expressed adequately by the post-Renaissance Bruno because the time for their full development had not yet arrived during the Renaissance; likewise, Dinant's ideas were a natural development of Avicebron's thought, which itself came too early to be effectively deployed.
136. Avicebron, *The Font of Life*, trans. John A. Laumakis (Milwaukee: Marquette University Press, 2014), 78.
137. "Everything in the same matter." This does not appear to be a quote from David of Dinant but rather Bloch's paraphrase of his ontology.
138. "Development": *Weltbildung*.
139. See Giordano Bruno, *Cause, Principle and Unity*, trans. R. J. Blackwell and Robert de Lucca (Cambridge: Cambridge University Press, 1998), 81; which renders this literally: "without act, without virtue and perfection."
140. See Bruno, 86. The passage's final sentence does not appear in Bruno's text but rather paraphrases his argument's central thrust.
141. Bruno, 61.
142. "Sublated": *Aufgehoben*.
143. Bloch cites *Georg Friedrich Wilhelm Hegel's Werke: Vollständige Ausgabe*, (Berlin: Duncker & Humblot, 1836), 15:232, the source text for Haldane and Simpson's 1896 translation of the *Lectures on the History of Philosophy*, which we have emended slightly; G. F. W. Hegel, *Lectures on the History of Philosophy*, trans. E. S. Haldane and F. H. Simpson (1896; New York: Humanities, 1983), 3:127. This passage is truncated in the Meiner edition upon which Robert Brown's 2009 Oxford edition is based; see G. F. W. Hegel, *Vorlesungen über die Geschichte der Philosophie*, ed. P. Garniron and Walter Jaeschke (Hamburg: Meiner, 1986), 3:65; G. W. F. Hegel, *Lectures on the History of Philosophy, 1825-6*, ed. and trans. Robert Brown (New York: Oxford University Press, 2009).
144. "Unity" is translated from *Sacheinheit*; this term does not appear in German translations of Spinoza but is rather the standard translation of Duns Scotus's *unitas realis* (real unity). Gunnar Hindrichs has suggested in personal correspondence that Bloch's use of *Sacheinheit* is meant to contrast Spinoza's *deus sive natura* with Descartes's *unitas compositionis* (unity of composition) of the *res extensa* and *res cogitans*.

145. See G. W. von Leibniz on "preformed seeds" in his *Principles of Nature and Grace, Based on Reason*, in *Philosophical Essays*, trans. Roger Ariew and Daniel Garber (Indianapolis: Hackett, 1989), 209ff.
146. Bloch misidentifies his source as Lichtenberg. The sentence is from Jean Paul, *Flegeljahre*, in *Werke*, ed. G. Lohmann (München: Hanser, 1963), 2:687. Several similar passages can be found in Lichtenberg; see, e.g., Georg Christoph Lichtenberg, *Philosophical Writings*, ed. and trans. Steven Tester (Albany: SUNY Press, 2012), 69; Georg Christoph Lichtenberg, *The Waste Books*, trans. R. J. Hollingdale (New York: New York Review of Books, 1990), 66. Thanks to Steven Tester and Kirk Wetters for their help in identifying Bloch's reference.
147. According to *The Encyclopedia of Islam*, vol. 3 (Mif-Naz), ed. C. E. Bosworth et al. (Leiden: Brill, 1993), there were no book burnings in Baghdad during Caliph al-Muqtafi's reign (1136–1160), although there were several under his successors, particularly Caliph al-Nasir Li-Din Allah (r. 1180–1225); see the entry on the latter, esp. sec. 7. Book burnings should not necessarily be taken to reflect the general obscurantism Bloch ascribes to them, however, as they were often symbolic affairs reflecting local political struggles rather than grand antiphilosophical actions; in personal correspondence, Dimitri Gutas wrote that they "had little substantive significance and even less influence." For a discussion of the context of book burnings in contemporary Andalusia, see Janina M. Safran, "The Politics of Book Burning in al-Andalus," *Journal of Medieval Iberian Studies* 6, no. 2 (June 2014): 148–68. Bloch's characterization of the period after Avicenna as being fundamentally hostile to philosophy is flawed; see Dimitri Gutas, "The Heritage of Avicenna: The Golden Age of Arabic Philosophy, 1000–ca. 1350," in *Avicenna and His Heritage*, ed. Jules Janssens and Daniel De Smet (Leiden: Leiden University Press, 2002), 81–97.
148. Almohad Caliph Abu Yusuf Yaqub al-Mansur (r. 1184–1199). Averroës fell out of favor in 1195, and his philosophical works (but not his scientific ones) were burned; he was rehabilitated a year and a half later. For a detailed account, see Émile Fricaud, "Le problème de la disgrâce," in *Averroès et l'averroïsme*, ed. André Bazzana, Nicole Bériou and Pierre Guichard (Lyon: Presses Universitaires de Lyon, 2005), 155–90; see also Safran, "The Politics of Book Burning," 162–65.
149. See *The Arabian Nights: Vol. 1*, ed. R. Irwin (New York: Penguin Classics, 2010), 545, where Avicenna's medical canon is called "senseless talk."
150. Galileo was found guilty of heresy in 1633 and sentenced to house arrest for the rest of his life. Bloch's friend Bertolt Brecht dramatized these events in his play *Leben des Galilei*.

151. A reference to the work of Mulla Sadra, or Sadr ad-Din Muhammad Shirazi (ca. 1571–1640), a Persian philosopher and theologian.
152. Al-Azhar University. We replace Bloch's "past century" with "nineteenth century."
153. "Earthly world:" *Diesseits*.
154. Quoted in the French; see Ernest Renan, *Averroës et l'Averroisme* (Paris: Michel Levy Frères, 1866), 86.
155. **Bloch's note on *mutakallimūn*: (That is, "teachers of kalam," the revealed word).** See note 125 here. On Ghazali's occasionalism, see Taneli Kukkonen, "Creation and Causation," in Pasnau, *The Cambridge History of Medieval Philosophy*, 236–37 and passim.
156. Quoted in the French; see Renan, *Averroës et l'Averroisme*, 108.
157. "To sublate": *Aufheben*.
158. *Sittlichkeit*.
159. I.e., normative elements.
160. See, e.g., Moses Maimonides, *The Guide of the Perplexed*, trans. Shlomo Pines (Chicago: University of Chicago Press, 1974), 1:54.
161. Peter Abelard (1079–1142) was a French philosopher and theologian.
162. "Imaginable": *nur möglichen*, literally "only possible."
163. Benedict de Spinoza (1632–1677) was a Dutch philosopher; see his *Theological-Political Treatise*, ed. Jonathan Israel (Cambridge: Cambridge University Press, 2007).
164. "Humanity": *Humanum*.
165. "All the better": *adäquater*, literally "more adequate."
166. "According-to-what-is considered-possible," "what-may-become-possible," and "objective Possibility": *nach Massgabe des Möglichen*, *In-Möglichkeit-Sein*, and *objektive Möglichkeit*, respectively.
167. *Figurbildungen*.
168. *Auszugsgestalten*. This and *Figurbildungen* are two of Bloch's terms for discernible elements of the not yet in the process of becoming, which he also calls *Prozessfiguren*, "process figures"; see Bloch, *Experimentum Mundi*, 155.
169. "Totum" is Bloch's term of art for the fulfilled totality toward which he holds human striving aims.
170. "The sheer desire to become": *lauter Werdelust*.
171. *In nuce*: "in a nutshell."
172. Jakob Böhme (1575–1624) was a German theologian and mystic. This translation from *The Holy Family* is from Karl Marx and Frederick Engels, *Collected Works* (New York: International, 1975), 4:128; "primary" translates from *primitiven*; perhaps "unsophisticated" would be better. We retain Marx's italicization, which Bloch ignores; in the original text,

furthermore, Marx makes a paragraph breaks after "species." Bloch cites the *Marx Engels Gesamtausgabe* 3:304ff.
173. In Ptolemaic cosmology, the earth existed as a lesser sphere within the celestial sphere of the universe.
174. "Totality-Statics": *Ganzheit-Statik*. Nicholas of Cusa (1401–1464) was a German philosopher and theologian; see his *Trialogus de Possest*, in Jasper Hopkins, *A Concise Introduction to the Philosophy of Nicholas of Cusa*, 2nd ed. (Minneapolis: University of Minnesota Press, 1980), 61–153. We have replaced Bloch's "Posset" with "Possest," Nicholas of Cusa's Latin neologism.
175. "Universal-Life": *All-Leben*.
176. "Processual labor and wealth of shapes": *Prozessmühe und Gestaltenfülle*.
177. In other words, Bloch suggests that Hegel almost transcended the Aristotelian Statics of perfect circles by temporalizing it in his theory of *Geist*'s progressive unfurling in history.
178. The German section heading is *Kunst, die Stoff-Form entbindend*. The closest English cognate to *entbinden* is "to unbind," but the word also connotes birth; childbirth is *Entbindung*. Depending on context, we have also translated it as "liberating" or "emancipating" in this final section.
179. "Entertaining and lending significance": *eines unterhaltend-bedeutenden*.
180. Gottfried Ephraim Lessing, *Emilia Galotti*, in *"Nathan The Wise," "Minna von Barnhelm," and Other Plays and Writings*, 79.
181. Arthur Schopenhauer, *The World as Will and Representation*, ed. and trans. Judith Norman, Alistair Welchman, and Christopher Janaway (Cambridge: Cambridge University Press, 2010), 1:248. Schopenhauer's emphasis, neglected by Bloch, has been maintained.
182. Georg Wilhelm Friedrich Hegel, *Aesthetics: Lectures on Fine Art*, trans. T. M. Knox (Oxford: Clarendon, 1975), 1:153. Bloch truncates and takes stylistic liberties with Hegel's original.
183. See note 98 here.
184. Julius Caesar Scaliger (1484–1558) was an Italian humanist.
185. Cf. Ernst Bloch, *The Principle of Hope*, trans. Neville Plaice, Steven Plaice, and Paul Night (Cambridge, MA: MIT Press, 1986): "Precisely this entelechetically or, as Aristotle also says, typically resolving force is powerfully remembered afresh in Engels' statement that realistic art is representation of typical characters in typical situations. Whereby the typical in Engels' definition obviously does not mean the average, but the significantly characteristic, in short, the essential image of the matter, decisively developed through exemplary instances" (216). See Frederick Engels, "Letter to Margaret Harkness, April 1888," in *Marx and Engels on Literature and Art* (Moscow: Progress, 1976), 90.

186. Quoted in Latin.
187. "The archetype of nature is altogether perfect in outline and proportions." See Frederick Morgan Padelford, *Select Translations from Scaliger's Poetics* (New York: Henry Holt, 1905), 53. Bloch quotes from Julius Caesar Scaliger, *Poetices libri septem* (Vincentia: Crispinus, 1561), 285 (book 3, chap. 25).
188. "Sought Typical": *erstrebbar Typische*.
189. It seems that Bloch means the parenthetical phrase to express the notion of entelechy; we have translated *Sache* ("thing," "matter") as "issue" to convey something in process of being born.
190. **Bloch's note: Cf. *On Poetry*, p. 14.** See Padelford, *Select Translations*, 19ff.
191. *Diderots Versuch über die Malerei*, in Johann Wolfgang Goethe, *Sämtliche Werke nach Epochen seines Schaffens*, ed. Karl Richter (München: Carl Hanser Verlag, 1991), 7:527.
192. *Dies Wichtigste*.
193. Aristotle, *De Anima*, trans. D. W. Hamlyn (Oxford: Clarendon, 1993), 60.
194. Aristotle, 9.
195. Aristotle, *Metaphysics*, trans. W. D. Ross, in *The Complete Works of Aristotle*, ed. J. Barnes (Princeton: Princeton University Press, 1984), 2:1683.
196. "Theoretical" replaces Horten's translation (Avicenna, *Die Metaphysik*) of "speculative."
197. Horten translates *ilm ilahi* as *Metaphysik*, while Marmura (in Avicenna, *The Metaphysics of the Healing*) translates it as "divine science"; in this particular passage, the latter is more accurate. See "Appendix D: Names for Aristotle's *Metaphysics* and Metaphysics as a Discipline in Avicenna's Works" in Amos Bertolacci, *The Reception of Aristotle's Metaphysics in Avicenna's Kitāb al-Šifāʾ* (Leiden: Brill, 2006), 593–606. "Metaphysics" is retained here in order to reflect Bloch's text. Horten adds the parenthetical "as a problem," which Bloch follows.
198. Bloch replaces Horten's *Mathematik* with *Metaphysik*. Horten's earlier translation differs considerably from Marmura's recent one; Horten's reads, "Metaphysics is the science that investigates the first causes of the Being of things belonging to the natural science and mathematics." This and similar divergences between the texts may be the result of different Avicennan manuscript sources; Marmura follows the C or Cairo edition, while Horten follows the L or Leiden edition. On this topic, see Bertolacci, *The Reception of Aristotle's Metaphysics*, appendix A; Amos Bertolacci, "The Doctrine of Material and Formal Causality in the *Ilahiyyat* of Avicenna's *Kitab al-Sifa*," *Quaestio* 2 (2002): 125–54, 54n1.
199. Bloch substitutes *ersten*, or "first," for *entferntesten*, or "ultimate," and paraphrases slightly.

200. Avicenna, *The Metaphysics of the Healing* (Marmura). Cf. Avicenna, *Die Metaphysik*, (Horten), 2–5, 22–23, 27. The variant Arabic readings that Marmura offers are used when they match Horten's German, which is used by Bloch.
201. Cf. Avicenna, *Die Metaphysik* (Horten), 269. Horten's passage emphasizes the passive potentiality of matter: "Every thing that comes into being, before its becoming, has either the {material} potential to exist, or else it is impossible."
202. Bloch slightly modifies Horten.
203. Cf. Avicenna, *Die Metaphysik* (Horten), 147.
204. Cf. Avicenna, *Die Metaphysik* (Horten), 138, which Bloch slightly emends.
205. Bloch follows Horten's *Dispositionen* and parenthetically addends *Anlagen*.
206. "In the manner of Aristotle."
207. *Causa materialis* follows Horten.
208. Myrobalan is defined in the *Oxford English Dictionary*: "The astringent plumlike fruit of any of various tropical trees of the genus *Terminalia* (family Combretaceae), esp. *T. bellirica* and *T. chebula*, formerly used medicinally but now chiefly in dyeing and tanning."
209. "Material cause" follows Bloch (following Horten), replacing Marmura's "the thing that bears potentiality."
210. Bloch (following Horten) concludes this passage with the following parenthetical clause: "and thus every process of change involves either one or more phases."
211. Cf. Avicenna, *Die Metaphysik* (Horten), 407–10.
212. Cf. Avicenna, *Die Metaphysik* (Horten), 600, which renders the last sentence differently: "If this is the case, then the form cannot be characterized as the cause of the {shaped, individualized, determined} matter, for form is at once both self-subsistent and independent of matter." Here, the book and chapter divisions in Horten's translation begin to diverge from those in Marmura's; Horten has 9.6 here, Marmura 9.4, a reflection of their different source manuscripts.
213. Bloch's translation (Horten) omits "unequal."
214. *Esse corpus*: "to be a body."
215. Cf. Avicenna, *Die Metaphysik* (Horten), 98–101.
216. "Grasp": *begreift*. "Predicables" describe how a subject may relate to a predicate; in other words, they describe how things may be classified. Aristotle's four predicables are definition, property, genus, and accident (*Topics* 1.4 [101b17–24]), which Porphyry's *Isagoge*, an influential third-century introduction to Aristotelian logic, revises as genus, species, difference, property, and accident. See Porphyry, *Isagoge*, ed. and trans.

Edward W. Warren (Toronto: Pontifical Institute of Mediaeval Studies, 1975); see also Edward W. Warren, introduction to *Isagoge*; cf. Christina D'Ancona, "Greek into Arabic," in Adamson and Taylor, *The Cambridge Companion to Arabic Philosophy*, 14–15.
217. "Intelligible": *begreifbaren*.
218. *Unbegreiflich*.
219. Averroës, *Tahafut al-Tahafut* (*The Incoherence of the Incoherence*), "First Discussion." Cf. Averroës, *Die Hauptlehren*, 30, which Bloch modifies significantly.
220. "Cannot . . . not-have-been": *kann . . . nicht nicht-gewesen*.
221. "Die Möglichkeit erfordert aber ein reales Ding, in dem sie inhäriert."
222. Horten's translation reads, "the possibility of the receiving principle [*des aufnehmenden Prinzips*]," i.e., the substratum's passive receptiveness to transformation. Van den Bergh's "agent" is *Ursache*, or "cause," in Horten's translation.
223. Bloch (Horten) renders Averroës more poetically: "There must therefore be present [in eternal Matter] an eternal movement which effectuates the succession in Matter of becoming and demising things, in an eternal chain."
224. Cf. Averroës, *Die Hauptlehren* (Horten), 104–5. Bloch slightly modifies Horten, who in this instance is clearer than Van den Bergh: "Potentiality requires a real thing in which it inheres. . . . The potentiality of the receptive principle (effect) is therefore a necessary condition for potentiality in a [material] cause, for a cause that cannot have an effect is impossible. . . . There must therefore be (in eternal matter) an eternal movement, which effectuates in matter the succession of the arising and demising things in an infinite chain, for 'arising' means the transformation and reshaping of a thing from potentiality to actuality. . . . Consequently it stands to reason that in the process of becoming, there is an eternal [*anfangslos*: literally "without beginning"] potentiality that exists as a substrate of the contrary, interchanging essential forms."
225. Aristotle, *Metaphysics* K.3 (1069b35–70a30).
226. "It does not give, but draws out."
227. *Suo genere*: "of its own kind."
228. "Actualizing principles": *das Aktualisierende*.
229. *Possibilität*, *Potenz*, *Möglichkeit*, and *Vermögen*, respectively.
230. Averroës, *The Incoherence of the Incoherence* (van den Bergh), 59 (1.101); cf. Averroës, *Die Hauptlehren* (Horten), 104. Bloch only cites elements of this passage's second sentence. It has been supplemented for the sake of clarity in English.

231. Bloch's note: Cf. Hegel, *Science of Logic*, *Werke*, [Berlin: Duncker und Humblot,] 1834, IV, S. 116; Philos.[ophische] Bibl.[iothek], 1923, S. 97: "When all the conditions of a fact are at hand, the fact steps into concrete existence." See G. W. F Hegel, *The Science of Logic*, trans. George di Giovanni (Cambridge: Cambridge University Press, 2010), 416 (11.321).
232. Averroës, *On Aristotle's Metaphysics*. Bloch cites (and slightly modifies) Averroës, *Die Metaphysik des Averroës: Nach dem arabischen übersetzt und erläutert*, trans. Max Horten (Halle, an der Saale: M. Niemeyer, 1912), 102–3.
233. "Something formed": *ein Geformtes*; "higher formed thing": *einem höher Geformten*.
234. Bloch cites Simon van den Bergh's translation of Averroës rather than Horten's; see Averroës, *Die Epitome Der Metaphysik des Averroës*, trans. Simon van den Bergh (Leiden: Brill, 1924), 25.
235. "The pregnant Possible": *des gehaltvoll Möglichen*.
236. "The One," translated from *Ur-Einen*, follows Stephen MacKenna's translation of ἕν—an essence that Plotinus claims is "beyond all statement," or impossible to articulate. Plotinus, *The Enneads*, trans. Stephen MacKenna (London: Faber & Faber, 1957), 395 (5.3.13). Bloch amends Richard Harder's German *Eine* (one) to *Ur-Einen*. See Plotinus, *Plotins Schriften*, vol. 1, trans. Richard Harder (Leipzig: Meiner, 1930). For Plotinus's description of "the One" in the present context, see Plotinus, *The Enneads*, 248 (3.8.10).
237. The *Weltgeist* (world spirit) to which Bloch refers, the Neoplatonist *anima mundi*, is usually rendered "world soul," as in the excerpt from Bruno's *Cause, Principle and Unity* further on. *Geist*, or "spirit," has Hegelian overtones and has been retained; in Harder's translation of Plotinus, *anima* is rendered *Seele*, not *Geist*.
238. Bloch's phrasing has been amended slightly for comprehension, for he here defies grammar, perhaps (read charitably) to reflect the ultimately ineffable nature of the One. A literal translation would read, "Precisely this empty, but also qualityless, impersonal," nominalizing each adjective to describe the *Ur-Einem*.
239. Bloch quotes from Plotinus, *Plotins Schriften*, 1:251. He amends the German slightly and adds several Greek terms in parentheses from the original.
240. *Usia* means "Being"; in Neoplatonism, it means "essence" or "substance."
241. "The unitary structure of the world": *einheitlichen Weltzusammenhangs*.
242. Bloch's note: Cf. [Hermann] Siebeck, *Unters[uchungen]. zur Philosophie der Griechen*, [Freiburg: 1888,] S. 181ff.
243. *Deus sive natura*: "God or Nature"; cf. Benedict de Spinoza, *Ethics*, trans. Edwin Curley (New York: Penguin, 1996), 114 (2.206–7): "That eternal and infinite being we call God, *or* Nature, acts from the same necessity of

nature from which he exists.... The reason, therefore, *or* case, why God, *or* Nature, acts, and the reason why he exists, are one and the same."
244. Solomon ibn Gabirol [Avicebron], *The Font of Life*, trans. John A. Laumakis (Milwaukee, WI: Marquette University Press, 2014). Bloch's text presumably offers his own German translations of the Latin; see Avicebron, *Fons Vitae*, in *Beiträge zur Geschichte der Philosophie des Mittelalters*, ed. Clemens Baeumker (München: Aschendorff, 1892–95), 1:226 (4.6). Bloch's German reads differently: "Since in the corporeal world all matter and all of its forms have a common essence, there is one matter and one form. In the same way, since in the intelligible world, all matter and all forms have a common essence, here too there is one matter and one form."
245. Cf. Avicebron, *Fons Vitae*, 1:227 (4.7). In this and the following Avicebron citations, Bloch leaves some elements in Latin.
246. Cf. Avicebron, *Fons Vitae*, 1:258 (5.1), 322 (5.35). Bloch here offers a paraphrase, using both German and Latin, of several passages on the cited pages.
247. Cf. Avicebron, *Fons Vitae*, 1:313 (5.30). The sentence preceding the Latin appears to be Bloch's rough paraphrase rather than a proper translation of Avicebron.
248. Cf. Avicebron, *Fons Vitae*, 1:13 (1.10). Bloch offers here a literal translation of the Latin.
249. See Aristotle, *Metaphysics* α.3 (995a).
250. Bloch replaces Kuhlenbeck's *bilden*, "to build, create," with *billigen*, "to affirm, endorse."
251. Bloch replaces *erschuf* with *schuf*.
252. "Matter ... stuff": *Materie ... Stoffe*; emphasis Bloch's.
253. "Der Erwecker," quoted from Giordano Bruno, *Gesammelte Werke*, trans. Ludwig Kuhlenbeck (Jena: Eugen Diederich, 1909), vol. 6. This work is better known by its Latin title, *Excubitor*. For the original, see Jordani Bruni Nolani [Giordano Bruno], *Opera Latine Conscripta*, trans. Francesco Fiorentino (Neapoli: D. Morano, 1879), 1.1.58–71. For an Italian translation by Barbara Amato, see E. C., "Iordani Bruni Nolani Camoeracensis Acrotismus: Una Traduzione Per Il 2000," *Bruniana & Campanelliana* 5, no. 1 (1999): 117–30.
254. "Vital materialists": *Stoffbeleber*, literally "matter invigorators."
255. Bruno, *Cause, Principle and Unity*, 61. Cf. Giordano Bruno, *Von der Ursache, dem Princip, und dem Einen*, trans. Adolf Lasson (Leipzig: Verlag der Dürr'schen Buchhandlung, 1902), 61.
256. The translation Bloch cites renders Bruno's *maghi*—here given in the English translation as "hermeticists"—as *Magiern* (mages), to which

Bloch addends *Persern* (Persians), thereby emphasizing the connection to Avicenna. Mages often represented hermetic knowledge; on this point specifically with reference to Bruno, see Francis Yates, *Giordano Bruno and the Hermetic Tradition* (Chicago: University of Chicago Press, 1991).

257. Bruno, *Cause, Principle and Unity*, 37–38; cf. Bruno, *Von her Ursache*, 29ff. Bloch slightly amends Lasson's German translation.
258. Lucretius (ca. 99–ca. 55 BCE) was a Latin Epicurean poet-philosopher. See Lucretius, *The Order of Things*, trans. A. E. Stalling (London: Penguin, 2007).
259. Bruno, *Cause, Principle and Unity*, 71. The "senators of Pallas's realm" are the philosophers (see 71*n*).
260. This work, once attributed to Duns Scotus, is no longer considered his; see Antonie Vos, *The Philosophy of John Duns Scotus* (Edinburgh: Edinburgh University Press, 2006), 106–10.
261. A more literal translation than "pure spirits" of *natura angelica* is "nature's angels."
262. "I return to the position of Avicebron."
263. See Jacob Böhme, *Aurora, oder Morgenröthe im Aufgang*, vol. 1 of *Sämtliche Schriften* (Stuttgart: Fromanns, 1955).
264. "Nature": *Sein*.
265. "Grand definition": *Grosse Bestimmung*, also "determination," hence a consequential claim.
266. "This side of advanced consciousness": *diesseits des fortgeschrittenen Bewusstseins*.

BIBLIOGRAPHY

Abu Sa'id-i Abu'l-Khayr. *Sukhanān-i manẓum-i Abu Sa'id-i Abu'l-Khayr*. Ed. Sa'id Nafisi. Tehran: Intishārāt-i Kitābkhāna-yi Shams, 1955.

Adamson, Peter, and Richard C. Taylor, eds. *The Cambridge Companion to Arabic Philosophy*. Cambridge: Cambridge University Press, 2005.

Adorno, Theodor. *Aesthetic Theory*. Trans. Robert Hullot-Kentor. Minneapolis: University of Minnesota Press, 1997.

———. "Blochs *Spuren*" [Bloch's Traces]. In *Noten zur Literatur*, 233–50. Frankfurt: Suhrkamp, 2002.

———. "On the Fetish Character in Music and Regression in Listening." In *The Essential Frankfurt School Reader*, ed. Andrew Arato and Eike Gebhardt, 270–99. New York: Continuum, 1994.

Adorno, Theodor, and Max Horkheimer. *Briefe und Briefwechsel*. Vol. I, *1928–1940*. Frankfurt: Suhrkamp, 1994.

Althusser, Louis. *Machiavelli and Us*. Ed. Francois Matheron. Trans. Gregory Elliott. London: Verso, 1999.

———. *Philosophy of the Encounter: Later Writings, 1978-1987*. Ed. Oliver Corpet and Francois Matheron. Trans G. M. Goshgarian. London: Verso, 2006.

———. "The Underground Current of the Materialism of the Encounter." In *Philosophy of the Encounter*, 163–207.

Anselm. *Proslogion*. Trans. Thomas Williams. Indianapolis: Hackett, 2001.

Aquinas, Thomas. *Aquinas Against the Averroists*. Trans. Ralph McInerny. West Lafayette, IN: Purdue University Press, 1993.

———. "God Is His Essence." Chap. 10 in *Compendium of Theology*. Trans. Richard J. Regan. Oxford: Oxford University Press, 2009.
———. *Summa Theologica*. New York: Benziger, 1948.
The Arabian Nights: Vol. 1. Ed. R. Irwin. Trans. Malcolm Lyons and Ursula Lyons. New York: Penguin Classics, 2010.
Aristotle. *The Complete Works of Aristotle*. 2 vols. Ed. J. Barnes. Princeton: Princeton University Press, 1984.
———. *De Anima*. Trans. D. W. Hamlyn. Oxford: Clarendon, 1993.
———. *Metaphysics*. In Barnes, *The Complete Works of Aristotle*, 2:1552–728.
———. *Metaphysics: Book Θ*. Trans. Stephen Makin. Oxford: Clarendon, 2006.
———. *Metaphysics: Books Z and H*. Trans. David Bostock. Oxford: Clarendon, 1994.
———. *On the Heavens*. In Barnes, *The Complete Works of Aristotle*, 2:447–511.
Averroës. *De Substantia Orbis*. Trans. Arthur Hyman. Cambridge, MA: Medieval Academy of America, 1986.
———. *Die Epitome Der Metaphysik des Averroës*. Trans. Simon van den Bergh. Leiden: Brill, 1924.
———. *Die Hauptlehren des Averroës nach seiner Schrift; Die Widerlegung des Gazali*. Trans. Max Horten. Bonn: Marcus & Weber Verlag, 1913.
———. *Die Metaphysik des Averroës: Nach dem arabischen übersetzt und erläutert*. Trans. Max Horten. Halle an der Saale: M. Niemeyer, 1912.
———. *Long Commentary on Aristotle's De Anima*. Ed. F. S. Crawford. Cambridge. MA: Medieval Academy of America, 1953.
———. *On Aristotle's "Metaphysics": An Annotated Translation of the So-Called "Epitome."* Ed. Rüdiger Arnzen. Berlin: De Gruyter, 2010.
———. *Tahafut al-Tahafut (The Incoherence of the Incoherence)*. Trans. Simon van den Bergh. London: Luzac, 1954.
Avicebron. *Fons Vitae*. In *Beiträge zur Geschichte der Philosophie des Mittelalters*. Vol. 1. Ed. Clemens Baeumker. München: Aschendorff, 1892–95.
———. *The Font of Life*. Trans. John A. Laumakis. Milwaukee: Marquette University Press, 2014.
Avicenna. *Die Metaphysik Avicennas, enthaltend die Metaphysik, Theologie, Kosmologie, und Ethik*. Trans. Max Horten. Halle an der Saale: R. Haupt, 1907; Frankfurt: Minerva, 1960.
———. *The Metaphysics of the Healing*. Trans. Michael Marmura. Provo, UT: Brigham Young University Press, 2005.
———. *The Physics of the Healing*. Trans. Jon McGinnis. Provo, UT: Brigham Young University, 2009.
———. *Réfutation de l'Astrologie*. Trans. Y. Michot. Beyrouth: Les Éditions Albouraq, 2006.

Baffioni, Carmela. "Metaphors of Light and the 'Verse of Light' in the Brethren of Purity." In *In the Age of al-Farabi*, ed. Peter Adamson, 163–77. London/Turin: Warburg Institute—Nino Aragno Editore, 2008.

Beiser, Frederick C. *The Fate of Reason*. Cambridge, MA: Harvard University Press, 1987.

———. "The Materialism Controversy." Chap. 2 of *After Hegel: German Philosophy 1840–1900*. Princeton: Princeton University Press, 2014.

Bennett, Jane. *Vibrant Matter*. Durham, NC: Duke University Press, 2010.

Berman, Marshall. *All That Is Solid Melts into Air*. New York: Verso, 2010.

Bertolacci, Amos. "The Doctrine of Material and Formal Causality in the *Ilahi-yyat* of Avicenna's *Kitab al-Sifa*." *Quaestio* 2 (2002): 125–54.

———. *The Reception of Aristotle's Metaphysics in Avicenna's Kitāb al-Šifā*. Leiden: Brill, 2006.

Bloch, Ernst. *Atheism in Christianity*. New York: Herder & Herder, 1972; London: Verso, 2009.

———. *Avicenna und die Aristotelische Linke*. Berlin: Rütten & Loening, 1952.

———. *Briefe*. 2 vols. Frankfurt: Suhrkamp, 1985.

———. *Das Materialismusproblem*. 1972. Vol. 7 of *Gesamtausgabe*.

———. *Das Prinzip Hoffnung*. Vol. 5 of *Gesamtausgabe*.

———. *Ernst Blochs Wirkung: ein Arbeitsbuch zum 90. Geburtstag*. Frankfurt: Suhrkamp 1975.

———. *Experimentum Mundi*. 1975. Vol. 15 of *Gesamtausgabe*.

———. *Gesamtausgabe*. 17 vols. Frankfurt: Suhrkamp, 1977.

———. *The Heritage of Our Times* Trans. Neville and Steven Plaice. Oxford: Blackwell, 1991.

———. *Man on His Own: Essays in the Philosophy of Religion*. Trans. E. B. Ashton. New York: Herder & Herder, 1970.

———. *Natural Law and Human Dignity*. Trans. Dennis Schmidt. Cambridge, MA: MIT Press, 1987.

———. *On Karl Marx*. London: Verso, 2018.

———. *A Philosophy of the Future*. Trans. John Cumming. New York: Herder & Herder, 1970.

———. *The Principle of Hope*. 3 vols. Trans. Neville Plaice, Steven Plaice, and Paul Knight. Cambridge, MA: MIT Press, 1986.

———. *The Spirit of Utopia*. Trans. Anthony A. Nassar. Stanford, CA: Stanford University Press, 2000.

———. *Tendenz, Latenz, Utopie*. Frankfurt: Suhrkamp, 1978.

———. *Thomas Münzer als Theologe der Revolution*. Vol. 2 of *Gesamtausgabe*.

———. *Traces*. Trans. Anthony A. Nassar. Stanford, CA: Stanford University Press, 2006.

———. *The Utopian Function of Art and Literature: Selected Essays.* Trans. Jack Zipes and Frank Mecklenburg. Cambridge, MA: MIT Press, 1989.

Bobik, Joseph, ed. *Aquinas on Being and Essence.* South Bend, IN: University of Notre Dame Press, 1965.

Boccaccio, Giovanni. *The Decameron.* Trans. G. H. McWilliam. New York: Penguin, 1995.

Böhme, Jacob. *Aurora, oder Morgenröthe im Aufgang.* Vol. 1 of *Sämtliche Schriften.* Stuttgart: Fromanns, 1955.

Bostock, David. Introduction to *Aristotle: Metaphysics. Books Z and H.* Oxford: Oxford University Press, 1994.

Bouretz, Pierre. *Witnesses for the Future.* Baltimore: Johns Hopkins University Press, 2010.

Breckman, Warren. *Marx, the Young Hegelians, and the Origins of Radical Social Theory.* Cambridge: Cambridge University Press, 1998.

Brentano, Franz. *The Theory of Categories.* 1907. Trans. Roderick Chisholm and Norbert Guterman. The Hague: Martinus Nijhoff, 1981.

Bruno, Giordano. *Cause, Principle and Unity.* Trans. Richard J. Blackwell and Robert de Lucca. Cambridge: Cambridge University Press, 1998.

———. *Gesammelte Werke.* 6 vols. Trans. Ludwig Kuhlenbeck. Jena: Eugen Diederich, 1909.

———. *Opera Latine Conscripta.* Trans. Francesco Fiorentino. Neapoli: D. Morano, 1879.

———. *Von der Ursache, dem Princip, und dem Einen.* Trans. Adolf Lasson. Leipzig: Verlag der Dürr'schen Buchhandlung, 1902.

Claussen, Detlev. *Theodor W. Adorno: One Last Genius.* Trans. Rodney Livingstone. Cambridge, MA: Harvard University Press, 2008.

Cohn, Norman R. *The Pursuit of the Millennium.* New York: Oxford, 1970.

Colville, Jim. Introduction to *Two Andalusian Philosophers.* London: Kegan Paul, 1999.

Connolly, William. *A World of Becoming.* Durham, NC: Duke University Press, 2010.

Corbin, Henry. *Avicenna and the Visionary Recital.* Princeton: Princeton University Press, 1960.

Cusa, Nicholas of. *Trialogus de Possest.* In Jasper Hopkins, *A Concise Introduction to the Philosophy of Nicholas of Cusa,* 61–153. 2nd ed. Minneapolis: University of Minnesota Press, 1980.

D'Ancona, Christina. "Greek into Arabic." In Adamson and Taylor, *The Cambridge Companion to Arabic Philosophy,* 10–30.

Davidson, Herbert A. *Alfarabi, Avicenna, and Averroës, on Intellect.* New York: Oxford University Press, 1992.

Delanda, Manuel. *A New Philosophy of Society.* New York: Bloomsbury, 2006.

Dietschy, Beat, Doris Zeilinger, and Rainer Zimmermann, eds. *Bloch-Wörterbuch*. Berlin: De Gruyter, 2012.
Dyson, Henry. *Prolepsis and Ennoia in the Early Stoa*. Berlin: De Gruyter, 2009.
E. C. "Iordani Bruni Nolani Camoeracensis Acrotismus: Una Traduzione Per Il 2000." *Bruniana & Campanelliana* 5, no. 1 (1999): 117–30.
The Encyclopedia of Islam. Vol. 3 (Mif-Naz). Ed. Kate Fleet, Gudrun Krämer, Denis Matringe, John Nawas, and Everett Rowson. Leiden: Brill, 1993.
Engels, Frederick. *Anti-Dühring*. Moscow: Progress, 1969 [1878].
———. *Dialectics of Nature*. Moscow: Progress, 1964 [1883].
Fakhry, Majid. *Averroës (Ibn Rushd)*. Oxford: One World, 2008.
Fricaud, Émile. "Le problème de la disgrâce." In *Averroès et l'averroïsme*, ed. André Bazzana, Nicole Bériou and Pierre Guichard, 155–90. Lyon: Presses Universitaires de Lyon, 2005.
Geoghegan, Vincent. *Ernst Bloch*. London: Routledge, 1996.
Ghazālī, Abū Ḥāmid Muḥammad ibn Muḥammad al-. *The Incoherence of the Philosophers*. Trans. Michael Marmura. 2nd ed. Provo, UT: Brigham Young University Press, 2002.
Goethe, Johann Wolfgang von. *Faust, Part I*. Trans. David Constantine. London: Penguin, 2005.
———. *Faust I & II: Goethe's Collected Works*. Trans. Stuart Atkins. Princeton: Princeton University Press, 2014.
———. *Sämtliche Werke nach Epochen seines Schaffens*. 21 vols. Ed. Karl Richter. München: Carl Hanser Verlag, 1991.
Goldziher, Ignác. *Vorlesungen über den Islam*. Heidelberg: C. Winter, 1910.
Gutas, Dimitri. *Avicenna and the Aristotelian Tradition*. 2nd ed. Leiden: Brill, 2014.
———. "The Heritage of Avicenna: The Golden Age of Arabic Philosophy, 1000–ca. 1350." In *Avicenna and His Heritage*, ed. Jules Janssens and Daniel De Smet, 81–97. Leiden: Leiden University Press, 2002.
———. "Origins in Baghdad," in Pasnau, *The Cambridge History of Medieval Philosophy*, 9–25.
Habermas, Jürgen. "Ernst Bloch: A Marxist Schelling." In *Philosophical-Political Profiles*, 61–78. Trans. Frederick G. Lawrence. Cambridge, MA: MIT Press, 1983.
Hankinson, R. J. "Stoic Epistemology." In *The Cambridge Companion to Stoicism*, ed. Brad Inwood, 59–84. Cambridge: Cambridge University Press, 2003.
Harman, Graham. *Tool-Being: Heidegger and the Metaphysics of Objects*. Chicago: Open Court, 2002.
Hegel, Georg Wilhelm Friedrich. *Aesthetics: Lectures on Fine Art*. Vol. 1. Trans. T. M. Knox. Oxford: Clarendon, 1975.
———. *Georg Friedrich Wilhelm Hegel's Werke: Vollständige Ausgabe*. 18 vols. Berlin: Duncker & Humblot, 1836.

———. *Lectures on the History of Philosophy*. 3 vols. Trans. E. S. Haldane and F. H. Simpson. New York: Humanities, 1983.
———. *Lectures on the History of Philosophy, 1825–6*. Ed. and trans. Robert Brown. 3 vols. New York: Oxford University Press, 2009.
———. *The Science of Logic*. Trans. George di Giovanni. Cambridge: Cambridge University Press, 2010.
———. *Vorlesungen über die Geschichte der Philosophie*. Ed. P. Garniron and Walter Jaeschke. 3 vols. Hamburg: Meiner, 1986.
Hesiod. *Works and Days*. In *Hesiod and Theognis*, l: 93–99. Trans. Dorothea Wender. London: Penguin, 1973.
Hudson, Wayne. *The Marxist Philosophy of Ernst Bloch*. London: St. Martin's, 1982.
Humboldt, Alexander von. *Cosmos*. Trans. E. C. Otté. London: Longman, Brown, Green and Longmans, 1849.
Ibn Gabirol, Solomon [Avicebron]. *The Font of Life*. Trans. John A. Laumakis. Milwaukee, WI: Marquette University Press, 2014.
Ibn Rushd's Metaphysics. Trans. Charles Genequand. 1499. Leiden: Brill, 1984.
Ibn Tufayl. *Ibn Tufayl's Hayy Ibn Yaqzan: A Philosophical Tale*. Trans. Lenn Goodman. Chicago: University of Chicago Press, 2009.
———. *Naturmensch, oder Geschichte des Hai Ebn Joktan: Ein morgenländischer Roman*. Berlin and Stettin: F. Nicolai, 1783.
———. *Philosophus Autodidactus, sive, Epistola Abi Jaafar ebn Tophail de Hai ebn Yokdhan*. Oxford: H. Hall, 1671.
Jamal, Mahmood, ed. and trans. *Islamic Mystical Poetry: Sufi Verse from the Early Mystics to Rumi*. London: Penguin, 2009.
Jean Paul. *Flegeljahre*. In *Werke: Vol. 2*. Ed. G. Lohmann. München: Hanser, 1963.
Jung, Werner. "Vor-Schein." In Dietschy, Zeilinger, and Zimmermann, *Bloch-Wörterbuch*, 664–72.
Kukkonen, Taneli. "Creation and Causation." In Pasnau, *The Cambridge History of Medieval Philosophy*, 236–37.
Ladurie, Emmanuel Le Roy. *Montaillou*. Trans. Barbara Bray. New York: Penguin, 1990.
Latour, Bruno. "On Actor-Network Theory: A Few Clarifications." *Soziale Welt*, 47, no 4 (1996): 369–81.
Leaman, Oliver, and Sajjad Rizvi. "The Developed *Kalam* Tradition." In *The Cambridge Companion to Classical Islamic Theology*, ed. Tim Winter, 77–98. Cambridge: Cambridge University Press, 2008.
Leibniz, Gottfried Wilhelm von. *Principles of Nature and Grace, Based on Reason*. In *Philosophical Essays*. Trans. Roger Ariew and Daniel Garber. Indianapolis: Hackett, 1989.

Lenin, Vladimir I. *Materialism and Empirio-Criticism*. 1909. In *Lenin: Collected Works*, vol. 14. Moscow: Progress, 1972.
Lessing, Gottfried Ephraim. *Emilia Galotti*. In *"Nathan the Wise," "Minna von Barnhelm," and Other Plays and Writings*, ed. Peter Demetz. New York: Continuum, 1991.
———. *Nathan the Wise*. In *"Nathan the Wise," "Minna von Barnhelm," and Other Plays and Writings*, ed. Peter Demetz, 173–276. New York: Continuum, 1991.
Lichtenberg, Georg Christoph. *Philosophical Writings*. Ed. and trans. Steven Tester. Albany: SUNY Press, 2012.
———. *The Waste Books*. Trans. R. J. Hollingdale. New York: New York Review of Books, 2000.
Logan, George M., and Robert M. Adams. Introduction to *Utopia*, by Thomas More. Cambridge: Cambridge University Press, 1989.
Long, A. A., and D. N. Sedley. *The Hellenistic Philosophers*. Vol. 1. Cambridge: Cambridge University Press, 1987.
Lorris, Guillaume de, and Jean de Meun. *The Romance of the Rose*. Trans. F. Horgan. Oxford: Oxford University Press, 1994.
Lucretius. *The Order of Things*. Trans. A. E. Stalling. London: Penguin, 2007.
Maier, Anneliese. *An der Grenze von Scholastik und Naturwissenschaft*. Rome: Edizioni di Storia e Letteratura, 1952.
Maimonides, Moses. *The Guide of the Perplexed*. Vol. 1. Trans. Shlomo Pines. Chicago: University of Chicago Press, 1974.
Marcolini, Patrick. "Le *De Tribus Impostoribus* (*Traité des 3 imposteurs*) et les origines arabes de l'athéisme philosophique européen." *Les Cahiers de l'ATP* (October 2003).
Marcus Aurelius. *Meditations*. In *Marcus Aurelius*. Trans. C. R. Haines. Cambridge, MA: Harvard Loeb Library, 1916.
Marcuse, Herbert. *The Aesthetic Dimension*. Boston: Beacon, 1979.
———. *One-Dimensional Man*. Boston: Beacon, 1964.
Marenbon, John. "The Emergence of Medieval Latin Philosophy." In Pasnau, *The Cambridge History of Medieval Philosophy*, 26–38.
Markun, Sylvia. *Ernst Bloch*. Berlin: Rohwohlt, 1977.
Marmura, Michael E. "Avicenna and the *Kalam*." In *Probing in Islamic Philosophy*, 95–130. Binghamton: SUNY Press, 2005.
Marx, Karl. *Economic and Philosophic Manuscripts*. In McLellan, *Karl Marx: Selected Writings*, 83–120.
———. *Karl Marx: Selected Writings*. Ed. David McLellan. Oxford: Oxford University Press, 1977.
———. "Theses on Feuerbach." In McLellan, *Karl Marx*, 171–74.
Marx, Karl, and Frederick Engels. *Collected Works*. Vol. 4. New York: International, 1975.

———. *Marx and Engels on Literature and Art*. Moscow: Progress, 1976.
McGinnis, Jon. *Avicenna*. Oxford: Oxford University Press, 2010.
Miller, J., and M. Miller. "*Voprosy Filosofi* (*Problems of Philosophy*), 3 (1948)." *Soviet Studies* 1, no. 3 (January 1950): 210–30.
Miner, Robert C. "Aquinas on Habitus." In *A History of Habit: From Aristotle to Bourdieu*, ed. T. Sparrow and A. Hutchinson, 67–88. New York: Lexington, 2013.
Minois, Georges. *Le Traité des Trois Imposteurs: Histoire d'un livre blasphématoire qui n'existait pas*. Paris: Albin Michel, 2009.
Moggach, Douglas, ed. *The New Hegelians*. Cambridge: Cambridge University Press, 2006.
Morewedge, Parviz. Foreword to *The Metaphysics of Avicenna (Ibn Sina)*. New York: Columbia University Press, 1973.
Morton, Timothy. *The Ecological Thought*. Cambridge, MA: Harvard University Press, 2010.
Netton, Richard Ian. *Muslim Neoplatonists: An Introduction to the Thought of the Brethren of Purity*. London: Routledge, 2002.
Padelford, Frederick Morgan. *Select Translations from Scaliger's Poetics*. New York: Henry Holt, 1905.
Pagels, Elaine. *The Gnostic Gospels*. New York: Vintage, 1979.
Pasnau, Robert, ed. *The Cambridge History of Medieval Philosophy*. Rev. ed. Cambridge: Cambridge University Press, 2014.
———. Introduction to Pasnau, *The Cambridge History of Medieval Philosophy*, 1–8.
Plotinus. *The Enneads*. Trans. Stephen MacKenna. London: Faber & Faber, 1957.
———. *Plotins Schriften*. Vol. 1. Trans. Richard Harder. Leipzig: Meiner, 1930.
Porphyry. *Isagoge*. Ed. and trans. Edward W. Warren. Toronto: Pontifical Institute of Mediaeval Studies, 1975.
Prigogine, Ilya, and Isabelle Stengers. *Order Out of Chaos*. Toronto: Bantam, 1984.
Proclus. *The Elements of Theology*. 2nd ed. Trans. E. R. Dodds. Oxford: Clarendon, 1992.
Pseudo-Dionysius. *The Divine Names*. In *Pseudo-Dionysius: The Complete Works*. Trans. Paul Rorem. New York: Paulist Press, 1987.
Reeves, Marjorie. *Joachim of Fiore and the Prophetic Future*. New York: Sutton, 1999.
Renan, Ernest. *Averroës et l'Averroisme*. Paris: Michel Levy Frères, 1866.
Runciman, Steven. *A History of the Crusades*. Vol. 3. Cambridge: Cambridge University Press, 1987.
Safran, Janina M. "The Politics of Book Burning in al-Andalus." *Journal of Medieval Iberian Studies* 6, no. 2 (June 2014): 148–68.
Said, Edward. *Orientalism*. New York: Vintage, 1979.
Scaliger, Julius Caesar. *Poetices libri septem*. Vincentia: Crispinus, 1561.
Schmauder, Andreas. "Der Arme Konrad in Württemberg und im badischen Bühl." In *Bundschuh: Untergrombach 1502, das unruhige Reich und die*

Revolutionierbarkeit Europas, ed. P. Blickle and T. Adam, 183–94. Stuttgart: Franz Steiner Verlag, 2004.

Schmidt, Alfred. *The Concept of Nature in Marx*. Trans. Ben Fowkes. London: New Left, 1971.

Schopenhauer, Arthur. *The World as Will and Representation*. Vol. 1. Ed. and trans. Judith Norman, Alistair Welchman, and Christopher Janaway. Cambridge: Cambridge University Press, 2010.

Siebeck, Hermann. *Untersuchungen zur Philosophie der Griechen*. Freiburg: Mohr, 1888.

Siebers, Johan. "Novum." In Dietschy, Zeilinger, and Zimmermann, *Bloch-Wörterbuch*, 633–64.

Spinoza, Benedict de. *Ethics*. Trans. Edwin Curley. New York: Penguin, 1996.

———. *Theological-Political Treatise*. Ed. Jonathan Israel. Trans. Michael Silverthorne and Jonathan Israel. Cambridge: Cambridge University Press, 2007.

Stepelevich, Lawrence, ed. *The Young Hegelians: An Anthology*. Cambridge: Cambridge University Press, 1997.

Strayer, Joseph. *The Albigensian Crusades*. New York: Oxford, 1970.

Tales from the Thousand and One Nights. Ed. W. Harvey. New York: Penguin, 1973.

Thompson, Peter, and Slavoj Žižek, eds. *The Privatization of Hope*. Durham, NC: Duke University Press, 2013.

Toews, John. *Hegelianism*. Cambridge: Cambridge University Press, 1980.

Vos, Antonie. *The Philosophy of John Duns Scotus*. Edinburgh: Edinburgh University Press, 2006.

Unseld, Siegried, ed. *Ernst Bloch zu Ehren: Beiträge zu seinem Werk*. Frankfurt: Suhrkamp, 1965.

Wiggershaus, Rolf. *The Frankfurt School*. Trans. Michael Robertson. Cambridge, MA: MIT Press, 1994.

Wisnovsky, Robert. "Avicenna and the Avicennian Tradition." In Adamson and Taylor, *The Cambridge Companion to Arabic Philosophy*, 92–136.

Wittner, Lawrence. *One World or None: A History of the World Nuclear Disarmament Movement Through 1953*. Stanford, CA: Stanford University Press, 1993.

Yates, Francis. *Giordano Bruno and the Hermetic Tradition*. Chicago: University of Chicago Press, 1991.

Zedler, Beatrice. Introduction to *On the Unity of the Intellect Against the Averroists*, by Thomas Aquinas. Milwaukee: Marquette University Press, 1968.

INDEX

Abstract utopia, xiv–xv, xvii
Abū-Sa'īd Abul-Khayr (sufi), 9
Active understanding, 16–18
Actuality, xvii, 23, 47–49, 53, 55, 82n97, 83n119, 91n224
Adorno, Theodor, xii, xiii, xxii, 72n38
Aeneid (Virgil), 62
Aesthetic realism, 45
Albigensians, 29, 76n36
Alexander of Aphrodisias, 13, 15, 19–20, 78n59
Alexander of Hales, 26–27
Alexander VI (Pope), 81n83
Alive, Son of Awake (Ibn Tufayl), 11, 13, 36
Althusser, Louis, xxiv
Amalric of Bena, 29
Anselm of Canterbury, 7, 75n29
Antichurch, Aristotelian Left and, 29–33
Anti-Dühring (Engels), xvi
Aquinas, Thomas, xx, xxi, 3, 19, 23–28, 75n29, 80n76, 81n83
Arendt, Hannah, xxiv
Aristotelianism, xx–xxi, 15, 45
Aristotelian Left, 16, 25; antichurch and, 29–33; Avicebron and, 58; Bruno and, 32; Hegel and, 14; matter and, xxi–xxii
Aristotelian Right, 16, 25
Aristotle: Averroës and, 7; Avicenna and, 6–7, 14–23; Bruno on, 62; Christianity and, 7; entelechy and, xix, 20–21, 28, 38, 81n91; on form, xvii–xviii; four causes, 83n114; four predicables of, 91n216; Islam and, xi, xx–xxi; on matter, xvii, 81n90; *Metaphysics*, xvii, 47, 53–55, 81n91; Neoplatonism and, 87; nonmechanistic matter and, 37–38; *On the Soul*, 47; *Physics*, 81n91; soul and, 17; transcendentalism and, 26; transformation of, 38–42
Art, 42–45
Atomism, 35
Averroës, xi, xii, xx, xxi, 3, 6; Aristotle and, 7; *Averroës on Aristotle's Metaphysics*, 53–56; book burnings of, 86n148; *The Incoherence of the Incoherence*, 13, 23, 52–53, 78n59; matter and, 22–23; persecution, 78n62; Qur'an and, 78n62
Averroism, 26–27, 29, 33, 44, 84n131
Avicebron (Ibn Gabirol, Solomon), xi, xx, 15, 64; *Fons Vitae*, 30–31, 57–59

Avicenna, xi, xii; Aquinas and, 23–28; Aristotle and, 6–7, 14–23; birth and background of, 1; book burnings of, 34, 86n147; ecstasy of, 13; education of, 1, 74n3; on metaphysics, 2, 21, 47–52, 90n212; mysticism of, 13; Qur'an and, 16; writings of, 2, 74n6
Avicenna and the Aristotelian Left (Bloch), xx–xxvi
Awakener, The (Bruno), 59–61

Bacon, Roger, 5, 36, 75n24
Benjamin, Walter, xii
Bennett, Jane, xxiv
Bible, 25
Bloch, Ernst: Adorno on, xiii; *Avicenna and the Aristotelian Left*, xx–xxvi; capitalism and, xvi; conception of matter, xvii; entelechy and, xix; God and, xii; Habermas on, xiii; Hegel and, 88n177; Kracauer on, xii; language of, xxiii–xxiv; letters of, xxvi, 72n38; Marxism and, xxiii; materialism of, xii, xx, 72n38; philosophy of, xiii–xvi; possibility and, xviii–xix, xxii; *The Principle of Hope*, xiv, xxii; Scheler on, xii; Schmidt and, xxv; *The Spirit of Utopia*, xiii, xiv; utopia and, xiv, xv, xxiii; utopianism of, xii–xiii; Weber and, xii; writings of, xii
Body, xxi, 16–17, 24, 29, 51–52
Böhme, Jakob, 39–40, 64
Brecht, Bertolt, 86n150
Brethren of Purity of Basra, 8–9, 35
Brothers of the Free Spirit, 9
Bruno, Giordano, xi, xx, 3, 30, 40, 44, 67, 85n135; Aristotelian Left and, 32; on Aristotle, 62; *The Awakener*, 59–61; execution of, 80n70; Hegel and, 32; naturalism of, 31; *On the Nature of Things*, 63; pantheism of, 15

Capitalism, xvi, xxii
Catholicism, 24
Causality, 28, 35, 80n69
Celestial dynamics, 82n99
Chosroes I (Sasanian emperor), 75n21
Christianity, xxi, 7, 19, 75n20, 76n37
Cicero, 20, 80n81
Colville, Jim, 78n54, 78n58
Concrete utopia, xiv–xv, xvii, 66
Connolly, William, xxiv
Corporeality, 52, 93n244
Cosmos, God and, 27
Cult of Mithra, 75n20
Cunning of reason, 79n63

D'Abano, Pietro, 29, 84n131
David of Dinant, 29–30, 33, 85n135, 85n137
Da Vinci, Leonardo, 73n1
Delanda, Manuel, xxiv
Deleuze, Gilles, xxiv
Descartes, René, 85n144
Determinism, freedom and, xvi
De Tribus Impostoribus, 77n47
Dialectical matter, utopia and, xvi–xx
Dialectics of Nature (Engels), xvi
Dualism, 64
Duns Scotus, John, 64, 85n144
Dynamei-on, xxv–xxvi, 15–16, 20, 38, 41, 54, 66
Dynamis, 54

Eckhart, Meister, 8
Ecstasy, knowledge and, 13–14
Efficacy, matter and, 32–33
Elements, 82n98
Elias, Jamal, 76n43
Emanation theory, 18
Embodiment, 52
Emergence, 21–22, 23
Empiricism, 14
Engels, Friedrich, 87n172, 88n185; *Anti-Dühring*, xvi; *Dialectics of Nature*, xvi
Enlightenment, 10–11, 14, 19, 36
Enneads, The (Plotinus), 56–57
Entelechy, 15, 27, 88n185, 89n189; Aristotle and, xix, 20–21, 28, 38, 81n91; incomplete; 67
Eriugena, Scotus, 7
Essence, 27, 28, 49, 83n120
Ethics, 35, 36
Existence, xxii, 22, 28, 42–43, 47, 48, 51, 90n201
Exploitation of nature, xvi

INDEX 107

Faith, truth and, 7
Feuerbach, Ludwig, xvi
Fons Vitae (Avicebron), 30–31, 57–59
Form, 15; active, 21; actuality and, 47; Aristotle on, xvii–xviii; matter and, xviii, xx, xxi, xxiv, 16, 19–23, 25, 31–32, 37–38, 39–40, 42–45, 51, 56, 58–59, 62, 65, 73n1, 81n90, 90n212; relation and, 56; spirit and, 25; universal, 52, 58–59, 62
Frederick II (Holy Roman Emperor), 9
Freedom, xv, xvi, xix, 79n63

Galilei Galileo, 86n150
Al-Ghazali, *The Incoherence of the Philosophers*, 10, 34
Gnosticism, 76n37
God, xxi; Aquinas on, 28; Bloch and, xii; causality of, 28, 35; cosmos and, 27; essence of, 28; existence of,28; knowledge of, 36; matter and, 30, 84n133; nature and, 31, 93n243; ontological argument, 28, 84n122; perfection and, 41; spirit and, 30; supernatural and, 18; transcendental power of, 27; will of, xvii, 31, 32, 58; world and, xxii
Goethe, Johann Wolfgang von, 25, 40, 45
Goldziher, Ignác, 77n44
Guide of the Perplexed (Maimonides), 36

Habermas, Jürgen, xiii
Harman, Graham, xxiv
Heaven, 16, 26, 42
Hebrew Bible, 9
Hegel, Georg Wilhelm Friedrich, 14, 15, 32, 37, 44, 79n63, 88n177; *Science of Logic*, 92n231
Hell, xxi, 16, 17
Heresy, 19, 31, 86n150
Hindrichs, Gunnar, 85n144
History, xvii
Hobbes, Thomas, 40
Holy Family, The (Marx), 39, 87n172
Holy Spirit, 30
Hope, xiii–xvi, 71n10
Horkheimer, Max, xii, 72n38
Horten, Max, 78n59, 78n62, 89n198, 90n212
Humans, xiv, xv, xix, xxii, 16, 79n63

Ibn Gabirol, Solomon. *See* Avicebron
Ibn-Mansur, Nuh (Samanid emir), 2, 74n5
Ibn Sina. *See* Avicenna
Ibn Tufayl, 78n51, 78n58; *Philosophus Autodidactus*, 11–12, 36
Idealism, materialism and, 65
Incoherence of the Incoherence, The (Averroës), 13, 23, 52–53, 78n59
Incoherence of the Philosophers, The (Al-Ghazali), 10, 34
Intellect, xxi, 17–18, 62, 81n83
Islam, xi, xx–xxi, 8, 34
Islamism, 35

Jesus of Nazareth, 9, 36
Joachim of Fiore, 9, 29–30, 77n48
John of Jandun, 29, 84n131
Justinian (Roman emperor), 75n21

Kabbalah, 80n79
Kata to dynaton, xviii–xx, xxv, 20, 54
Knowledge, 6–11, 7, 13–14, 36, 75n27
Kracauer, Siegfried, xii

Languedoc, 76n36
Latour, Bruno, xxiv
Law of causality, 10
Leben des Galilei (Brecht), 86n150
Leibniz, 52
Lenin, Vladimir, xvi
Light, 7, 47
Lowe, Adolph, xxvi
Lukács, Georg, xii

Magnus, Albertus, xx, 7, 24, 30, 58, 81n83
Maimonides, 36
Al-Mansur, Abu Yusuf Yaqub (Almohad caliph), 86n148
Marcuse, Herbert, xxii
Marx, Karl, xi, xiv, xvi, 39, 41, 87n172
Marxism, xix, xxiii
Material cause, 49–51, 90n209
Materialism, xi, xii, xvi, xvii, xx, 40, 41, 63, 65, 73n45
Materialism and Empirio-Criticism (Lenin), xvi
Mathematics, 2, 48, 89n198

Matter, 63; activation of, 40; Aquinas on, 25; Aristotelian Left and, xxi–xxii; Aristotelian Right and, xxi; Aristotle and nonmechanistic, 37–38; Aristotle on, xvii, 81n90; Averroës and, 22–23; Avicenna and, xxiii; Bloch's conception of, xvii; body and, 51–52; common, 57; as eternal essence, 21; fecundity of, 41; form and, xviii, xx, xxi, xxiv, 16, 19–23, 25, 31–32, 37–38, 39–40, 42–45, 51, 56, 58–59, 62, 65, 73n1, 81n90, 90n212; God and, 30, 84n133; as inert, xvi, xvii; inner life of, 33; *nous* and, 15; potency of, 54–55; potentiality of, 16, 41, 47, 53, 90n201; qualities of, 39–40; Renaissance and, 42; spirit and, 30, 57–58; truth and, 45; as unfinished, 45; universal, 56, 58–59; utopia and, 42

Metaphysics (Aristotle), xvii, 47, 53–55, 81n91

Metaphysics of the Healing, The (Avicenna), 47–52

More, Thomas, xiii

Mortality, 61

Morton, Timothy, xxiv

Moses, 9, 36

Motion, 22, 39–40, 47, 50, 51, 53–54

Muhammad, 3–4, 6–7, 9, 36

Münzer, Thomas, 19, 81n85

Myrobalan, 50, 90n208

Mysticism, 8, 10, 12, 13

Naturalism, 8, 12, 15, 18, 31, 44, 78n62

Natural philosophy, 14

Natura naturans, xxv

Nature, xvi, xxv, 25, 31, 43, 44, 64–65, 80n69, 93n243

Neoplatonism, 6, 8, 9, 27, 56, 58, 75n20, 87, 92n237, 92n240

Neue, xiv

New Testament, 9

Nicholas of Cusa, 41

Nominalism, 24

Nous, 15, 57, 80n75

Novum, xiv, xvi

Objectivity, xviii, 37–38, 42

Obscurantism, 86n147

Old Testament. *See* Hebrew Bible

One, The (Plotinus), 57, 92n236, 92n238

On the Nature of Things (Bruno), 63

On the Soul (Aristotle), 47

Orpheus, 62

Orthodoxy, 12, 23, 34

Pantheism, xvi, xxi, 8, 13, 15, 31, 33, 40, 65, 78n62

Paul, Jean, 33

Philosophia Orientalis (Avicenna), 2, 12–13, 30

Philosophus Autodidactus (Ibn Tufayl). *See Alive, Son of Awake*

Physics (Aristotle), 81n91

Plotinus, 56, 57, 92n236

Plurality, 52–53

Poetics (Scaliger), 44

Political theory, materialism and, 73n45

Possibility, xv, xvii, xviii–xix, xx, xxii, xxv–xxvi, 37–39, 41–42

Potency, of matter, 54–55

Potentiality, xvii–xviii, 82n97, 83n106; actuality and, 48–49, 53, 55, 91n224; of matter, 16, 41, 47, 53, 90n201; passive, xxi, 20; of receptive principle, 91n224; of things, 91n224

Prigogine, Ilya, xxiv–xxv

Principle of Hope, The (Bloch), xiv, xxii

Ptolemy, 40–41, 88n173

Qur'an, 5, 8, 10, 12, 16, 36, 78n62

Realism, xiv, 45

Reality, xii, xiv, xv, xviii, xxii, 21, 82n97

Real possibility, xv, xvii

Reason, xxii, xxiii, 17–18, 35, 79n63

Receptive principle, 91n224

Religion, 10, 33–37

Renaissance, xxi, 41, 42

Resurrection, 16

Revolutionary politics, 79n63

Rituals, 4, 35

Robinson Crusoe (Defoe), 11

Romance of the Rose (de Lorris), 29

Roman Empire, xxiii, 18, 75n20

Scaliger, Julius Caesar, 44

Scheler, Max, xii

Schelling, Friedrich Wilhelm August, 65

Schmidt, Alfred, xxv

Scholasticism, 2, 23, 24, 26
Schopenhauer, Arthur, 43
Science, xiv, xv, 5, 34, 35
Science of Logic (Hegel), 92n231
Siger of Brabant, 26
Soul, xxi, 16–17, 24
Spinoza, Benedict de, 28, 33, 67, 85n144; *Theological-Political Treatise*, 36–37
Spirit, 25, 29, 30, 59, 60, 61
Spirit of Utopia, The (Bloch), xiii, xiv
Stengers, Isabelle, xxv
Stoicism, xxiii, 10, 18
Strato, 19, 58
Sufism, 8–9, 12

Tertullian, 7, 76n33
Theological-Political Treatise (Spinoza), 36–37
Theological virtues, 71n10
Theology, 5, 40
Thompson, Peter, xviii
Tolerance, 19, 36
Torah, 81n84

Universal forms, 52, 58–59, 62
Universal intellect, 62
Universal matter, 56, 58–59
Universal reason, xxiii, 17–18, 35–36
Universals, problem of, 24
Utopia: abstract, xiv–xv, xvii; Bloch and, xiv, xv, xxiii; concrete, xiv–xv, xvii, 66; dialectical matter and, xvi–xx; emancipation and, xiv; etymology of, xiii; hope and, xiii; Marx on, xvi; materialism and, xvii; matter and, 42; reality and, xii; unreality and, xiii
Utopianism, xii–xiii

Virgil, *Aeneid*, 62

Weber, Max, xii
What-is-considered-possible (*Nach-Möglichkeit-Sein*), xv, xviii–xx, 20, 37, 43, 54, 79n64, 87n166
What-may-become-possible (*In-Möglichkeit-Sein*), xviii–xx, 20, 37, 38, 43, 54, 79n64, 87n166

NEW DIRECTIONS IN CRITICAL THEORY

AMY ALLEN, GENERAL EDITOR

New Directions in Critical Theory presents outstanding classic and contemporary texts in the tradition of critical social theory, broadly construed. The series aims to renew and advance the program of critical social theory, with a particular focus on theorizing contemporary struggles around gender, race, sexuality, class, and globalization and their complex interconnections.

Narrating Evil: A Postmetaphysical Theory of Reflective Judgment, María Pía Lara

The Politics of Our Selves: Power, Autonomy, and Gender in Contemporary Critical Theory, Amy Allen

Democracy and the Political Unconscious, Noëlle McAfee

The Force of the Example: Explorations in the Paradigm of Judgment, Alessandro Ferrara

Horrorism: Naming Contemporary Violence, Adriana Cavarero

Scales of Justice: Reimagining Political Space in a Globalizing World, Nancy Fraser

Pathologies of Reason: On the Legacy of Critical Theory, Axel Honneth

States Without Nations: Citizenship for Mortals, Jacqueline Stevens

The Racial Discourses of Life Philosophy: Négritude, Vitalism, and Modernity, Donna V. Jones

Democracy in What State?, Giorgio Agamben, Alain Badiou, Daniel Bensaïd, Wendy Brown, Jean-Luc Nancy, Jacques Rancière, Kristin Ross, and Slavoj Žižek

Politics of Culture and the Spirit of Critique: Dialogues, edited by Gabriel Rockhill and Alfredo Gomez-Muller

Mute Speech: Literature, Critical Theory, and Politics, Jacques Rancière

The Right to Justification: Elements of Constructivist Theory of Justice, Rainer Forst

The Scandal of Reason: A Critical Theory of Political Judgment, Albena Azmanova

The Wrath of Capital: Neoliberalism and Climate Change Politics, Adrian Parr

Media of Reason: A Theory of Rationality, Matthias Vogel

Social Acceleration: A New Theory of Modernity, Hartmut Rosa

The Disclosure of Politics: Struggles Over the Semantics of Secularization, María Pía Lara

Radical Cosmopolitics: The Ethics and Politics of Democratic Universalism, James Ingram

Freedom's Right: The Social Foundations of Democratic Life, Axel Honneth

Imaginal Politics: Images Beyond Imagination and the Imaginary, Chiara Bottici

Alienation, Rahel Jaeggi

The Power of Tolerance: A Debate, Wendy Brown and Rainer Forst, edited by Luca Di Blasi and Christoph F. E. Holzhey

Radical History and the Politics of Art, Gabriel Rockhill

Starve and Immolate: The Politics of Human Weapons, Banu Bargu

The Highway of Despair: Critical Theory After Hegel, Robyn Marasco

A Political Economy of the Senses: Neoliberalism, Reification, Critique, Anita Chari

The End of Progress: Decolonizing the Normative Foundations of Critical Theory, Amy Allen

Recognition or Disagreement: A Critical Encounter on the Politics of Freedom, Equality, and Identity, Axel Honneth and Jacques Rancière, edited by Katia Genel and Jean-Philippe Deranty

What Is a People?, Alain Badiou, Pierre Bourdieu, Judith Butler, Georges Didi-Huberman, Sadri Khiari, and Jacques Rancière

Death and Mastery: Psychoanalytic Drive Theory and the Subject of Late Capitalism, Benjamin Y. Fong

Left-Wing Melancholia: Marxism, History, and Memory, Enzo Traverso

Foucault/Derrida Fifty Years Later: The Futures of Genealogy, Deconstruction, and Politics, edited by Olivia Custer, Penelope Deutscher, and Samir Haddad

The Habermas Handbook, edited by Hauke Brunkhorst, Regina Kreide, and Cristina Lafont

Birth of a New Earth: The Radical Politics of Environmentalism, Adrian Parr

The Practice of Political Theory: Rorty and Continental Thought, Clayton Chin

Queer Terror: Life, Death, and Desire in the Settler Colony, C. Heike Schotten

Naming Violence: A Critical Theory of Genocide, Torture, and Terrorism, Mathias Thaler

GPSR Authorized Representative: Easy Access System Europe, Mustamäe tee
50, 10621 Tallinn, Estonia, gpsr.requests@easproject.com

www.ingramcontent.com/pod-product-compliance
Lightning Source LLC
Chambersburg PA
CBHW021954290426
44108CB00012B/1069